CONTENTS

INTRODUCTION

Owning an Umbrella Cockatoo is a unique and specialized situation. They will test your nerves, your patience, your hearing, your skin tenacity, your blood volume, and your temper. They are extremely high-maintenance, and if you are unable to perform the required maintenance, the effects will turn your world upside down, and will have harmful ramifications for the bird in your care.

Adopting or purchasing an Umbrella Cockatoo is surprisingly akin to adopting a baby in every respect, except that the U2 will not move out at 18, nor will it take care of you when you get old. Instead, it will always need you, every single day, and it will live to a ripe old age of at least 60. The oldest on record was 110. So think about it beforehand. Think about it deeply and intensely. It is a life-changer.

If you do it right, and you provide the bird with what it needs, you will reap smiles, laughter and love every single day. Well, almost every single day. Do it wrong, and both you and the bird will pay a very high price.

Adopting a 'too is a bit like making a deal with the devil. You must do everything required, or your life can turn to h-e-double hockey sticks.

One of the first things I want to say is that I am not a scientist, or avian expert. I am just a woman who has been living and learning with a wonderful Umbrella Cockatoo named Benjamin. He chose the name by the way. When we bought him he was "about 2." There is no way of knowing whether that was his real age, so we really don't know how old he is. He is a non-flying Umbrella, though we did not know this when we bought him. Honestly, when we got him, we didn't know much about him, or about U2s in general.

Neither I nor my husband had ever had a bird before. Consequently, there was a big learning curve. In this book, I share what I have learned over the years, alongside Benjamin, who has been a marvelous teacher to me. In addition to what he has taught me, I have read books, surfed the internet for countless hours, and talked with avian veterinarians and other 'too owners. But a good half of this book is about the experience I have had as I diligently endeavored to create a happy life for Benjamin, my adorable U2. I will talk about my life with him, alongside factual data from informed sources.

Due to how I constructed our life together, I have had very few behavioral issues with Benjamin, so I cannot speak with authority on that. This is not meant as a "tell all" book, so I won't cover extensive physical or medical information. I will not breed Benji, so there will be no information about how to breed them, or how to raise baby 'toos, as I know nothing about that. I also think that there are plenty of birds in rescues, and there will be plenty more in the future – so I see breeding more of them into the world as a pretty selfish human endeavor, and a detriment to the birds. That comment will be my only rant in this book.

This book is mostly about what you are getting into if you buy an Umbrella Cockatoo, general daily life with them, and how to keep a happy 'too. In addition to the contents of this book, there is a Benjamin channel on YouTube, where I put up some videos of how he spends his days. The channel is called **Benjamin the Best Cockatoo**.

Umbrella Cockatoos are also known as White Cockatoos, Great White Crested Cockatoos, and U2s. I went into U2 ownership a blank slate. Benjamin was basically a mildly-researched impulse buy. (A pet purchase should never be an impulse buy!) The little bit of research I did beforehand was how I learned that they were loud and needy. But I figured I had a personality and lifestyle that could handle loud and needy.

Everything I read said that a U2 is definitely not a "first time bird." But I did it anyway. I think that while it is good advice, I also believe that it's more important that the adopting person or family is eagerly willing to learn, and do what needs to be done, rather than assuming only a previous bird owner will make a good U2 owner. Frankly, as I've learned how to care for Benjamin, I've also begun to understand that keeping a Cockatoo is barely similar to keeping most other birds. U2s are extremely unique – unique in how they think, how they handle relationships, and in how to keep them happy. Using a comparison coined by comedian Larry Miller, the difference between the needs of a Cockatoo and any other bird, is like the difference between shooting a bullet and throwing it.

As I was looking for books to read on Umbrella Cockatoos, nowhere did I find a book that really told me how to *live with* a U2. So Benjamin and I wanted to share our experience with people, to hopefully help others learn from our mistakes, and our successes. I tried to put together the book I wish had been available when I considered buying an Umbrella Cockatoo. This one will contain a few pictures and links to videos of my teacher, my mentor - my beautiful Benjamin.

So welcome to the world of Benji, and his U2 brothers and sisters. Thank you for joining us! We hope we can help you along on this journey.

Benjamin popping bubble wrap in his dining room play space, atop a cage he never, ever enters.

CONTEMPLATION

There are some things that you should know as you contemplate the purchase of an Umbrella Cockatoo.

1) The bird will be loud. If you, and **everyone** in your household, can run a chainsaw next to your ears for two minutes and still smile afterward, you will probably be fine. If you cannot, if you even flinch, you should think twice, or better yet, simply choose a quieter bird. The U2's scream can be heard 3 miles away. Like Nigel Tufnel's amplifiers in the classic 1984 comedy film, *This is Spinal Tap*, the U2 scream goes to 11 (and a Moluccan goes to 12!). When Benjamin screams while on my shoulder, it feels as if someone is ramming a screwdriver into my ear canal. It is probably the reason why the phrase, "What?" has become my response to almost everything my husband says, even when he's right next to me. The scream, and the songs, of a U2 are *very* loud. This should be noted if you live in an apartment or duplex and are thinking of getting a U2. Understand that it will absolutely, without question, bother the neighbors, and may even cause you to be served with an eviction notice. U2s are *not* designed for apartment living.

2) The bird will require a tremendous amount of your time. If you cannot, unquestionably, dedicate **several hours each day** to spending exclusive **out-of-the-cage time** with your bird, it is not the bird for you.

3) The bird will damage things. It will chew on anything and everything – wall corners, electrical cords, clothing, doors, window frames, ceramics, plants, baseboards, couches, tables, chairs, remote controls, computers, rugs, keyboards, cellphones... if the bird can get to it, at some point, the bird will chew on it. Because their beaks are powerful, whatever they chew on is often damaged, sometimes beyond repair,

instantaneously. You cannot train them to not chew. Chewing is their
life. It's in their DNA. It is what they do, and how they keep their beak
filed down. Dogs chase things. U2s chew. Fish swim. U2s
chew. Cats jump to high heights. U2s chew. The bird must spend a
good amount of time outside of its cage, so things will be damaged.
And they can cause this damage in a nanosecond, so don't think you can
stop it. There cannot be one U2 owner in the world who has not lost
something dear to them to the always-chewing beak of their bird. This
trait is also why they do not make good pets if you are living in a rental
unit of any kind. Guaranteed, you will *not* get your security deposit
back.

4) On average, U2s live to be 60-70 years old. Your bird will probably
   outlive you. You will have to come up with a transition plan for the
   bird.

5) The bird will require a very large cage, aviary, or a room in your home,
   and lots of toys throughout its life, for both entertainment and chewing
   purposes.

6) Avian veterinarians are not all that easy to come by, so you must make
   sure you have a good one within a comfortable travel distance of your
   home, and all your future homes.

7) Umbrella Cockatoos produce a powdery dander which can cause severe
   allergies and/or lung issues in many people. If you have allergies
   already, or any lung problems at all, this is not the bird for you. Their
   powder emanates from them every second of every day, coats
   everything around them, and floats around in the air 24/7. An air filter
   can cut down the amount, but it cannot stop it. Even a healthy person
   can develop an annoying cough after living with a U2 for a few years.

8) Because of their extreme needs, many U2s have been given up and re-
   homed several times before they are 3 years old. They are a highly
   difficult animal to keep, and should not be purchased with even a sliver

of doubt. The bird will suffer, and that's simply not fair.

9) Once an Umbrella Cockatoo hits sexual maturation around the age of 5, they can be highly unpredictable during breeding season. They are driven by their hormones, and have a strong desire to reproduce. They aren't making an intellectual choice, but are driven by an innate need - it is nature. Their personalities change thusly, for the entire breeding season (Dec – March). Males especially, are reputed to bite with abandon, and go on frequent rampages, making them dangerous for people, especially children, to be around. It can cause some male U2s to become extremely protective of their female handlers. Through this, their need for daily attention is still required.

If you feel you comprehend the gravity of the situation, and you think you can offer the bird a good home, your next step is choosing a bird. Umbrella Cockatoos will generally cost between $1,000 and $4,000. You can find a bird rescue or a breeder, go to a pet shop, or find one through classified ads.

I highly suggest going to an avian rescue, as there are so many thousands of birds in these rescues who need homes. As a bonus, the knowledgeable staff will be more helpful to you there than anywhere else. They will know the birds well, and can assist you in meeting the right bird for you. Bear in mind however, when it comes to Umbrella Cockatoos, rescues are understandably very discerning about who they will allow to adopt. They are faced with overflow numbers of these birds, because they require such specialized care, and so few people can really provide it. U2s are surrendered to rescues everyday. It is the responsibility of the staff to take measures to be assured that the bird is not faced yet again with another person or family who will abandon it to a rescue when they find they cannot care for it properly. So you must show them that you are ready, willing, able and prepared to care for the bird.

Using the classified ads can also be a good route, as you are generally buying the bird from its current owner, who will have direct knowledge of living with that particular bird, and can answer questions, as well as provide specific tips and advice - assuming they are truthful.

It is always a good idea to meet the bird before you buy it, but you can purchase a bird and live happily ever after without this step. (We did!)

The saddest aspect of the domesticated life of a Cockatoo is that they are not always appreciated and loved, mostly due to their often incessant loud screaming, especially when their needs are not being met. And the more miserable they are in their home environment, the louder and more often they scream, creating a vicious circle usually ending in the surrendering or selling of the bird. This also means that these same birds will scream mercilessly in their new homes, until someone teaches them that they do not have to scream to get what they need. Many will have been through numerous households, and will have lived less than happy, satisfactory lives. This will affect their personalities. These birds can still make lovely friends for you. It will simply take them longer to trust you, and you will need to work harder for that trust. But the bond for which you will work hard to achieve, and will finally experience, will be stronger than ever.

So if you are a patient and loving person, don't write off older, crankier birds. However, if you have small children, a large family, or a noisy, active family, it's best for everyone to choose a well-adjusted bird who will find it easier to handle chaos. That said, U2s feed off of the energy around them. Their need to connect is so strong that they will act accordingly to fit into a family. Consequently, if you have a chaotic family environment, you will probably have a constantly riled up bird who will scream a lot and potentially bite people without warning. This can make out-of-cage time difficult at best, and dangerous at worst. Truthfully, even a well-adjusted U2 would not be a good fit for that kind of environment. The best environment for a U2 is calm, quiet, and uneventful. Their native habitat is in large fields and high in tree tops in wooded areas, where nothing much is going on. Living in chaos and noise can be difficult on them.

I don't want to make people afraid, but I do think it should be made very clear: U2s have a very damaging bite, so keeping them around children is a danger. I am not going to say that it is 100% certain that a child would be bitten, but when hyper (which happens when children are running around having a good time, as children should be) the 'too could be inclined to bite, whether in aggression or play. So time with small children should always be supervised. In a mellow environment bites rarely happen. But in hyperactivity, it is a good 70/30 shot that a chomp is right around the corner. My Benjamin is the sweetest little bird, but can go from mellow to enjoying an amusing dance party with the neighbor children, and he is ready to bite someone before the dance is over. And then of course you have the increased potential for bites during breeding season. These can easily send a child or an adult to the emergency room.

Still thinking of getting one? Okay, let's move on.

It's a good idea to prepare for the arrival of your bird almost as if you were preparing for a new baby. Your bird has unique needs and it's best to be as ready as you can with the items that will be required.

Things you should have ready when you purchase an Umbrella Cockatoo:

* An aviary, bird cage, or a dedicated room.
An aviary, also known as a flight cage, is a very large bird cage, which gives the bird actual flying room. A bird cage (smaller than an aviary) should only be used if you plan to let the bird be out and about for a good number of hours each day. If you dedicate a room (which, in my opinion, is the best way to keep an Umbrella Cockatoo), and care at all about the room's future condition, all baseboards, window frames, and the door frame should be covered, or blocked with boxes, cabinets etc., or switched to metal versions. All outlets should be blocked, or better yet raised to a height unreachable from the floor and shelving. If the room is carpeted, I would strongly suggest that you buy some inexpensive laminate flooring and put that down over the carpet. It will be chewed apart, so plan on having back-up. Quarry tiles are also good flooring. The bottom of the door should be covered in metal, or the door itself replaced by a steel or composite door. You can also simply place a draft inhibitor at the base of the door to protect it, but it will be destroyed so you should have replacements on hand. Do not use a draft inhibitor that is filled with tiny beads.

*A great number of chewable toys. There are "parrot toys" available to hang in the cage, or you can make your own. Examples of good, inexpensive toys are:
Lincoln Logs
Tinker Toys
Popsicle sticks

Wooden clothespins
Plastic figurines
Sewing thread spools
Cedar blocks/planks/balls
Small tree branches
Soft wood in various shapes and sizes
Empty water bottles
Plastic sticks
Pumice stones
Cuttlebones
Foam rubber pads (poly-foam)
Small phone books
Print catalogs
Stuffed animals (avoid any filled with tiny beads)
Wicker baskets of any size
Cardboard boxes
Bubble wrap with small bubbles

Since many children's toys make great 'too toys, you can find a wonderful array of U2 toys at any thrift store, garage sale or clearance section of a retail store. As you would for a child, avoid toxic paints.

* Pelleted parrot food
Benjamin will only eat ZuPreem fruity pellets, but there are many varieties available. Check reviews or talk to knowledgeable store staff before buying, as some are less than stellar and don't have the needed nutrients. Mold and lack of variety in the bag seem to be the biggest problems. It's a good idea to check expiration dates on bags.

* Fresh fruits and vegetables
Never feed them avocados, onions, garlic or chocolate. But other than that, experiment to see what they will and will not eat. If using canned vegetables instead of fresh, use the 'no salt' versions.

* Plenty of paper towels
You will use these to clean up the bird poos, as well as the skins of fruits and vegetables. Most are not eaten in their entirety (fruits and veg, not poos), and parts will be left to be cleaned up post-meal. You can easily go through at least one roll of paper towels each week.

* Water bowl and food bowl
Not ceramic or glass as your bird will probably throw them around.

* Shallow tub at least 1' long (for bird baths), a shower perch, or a spray
bottle, if you wish to bathe or shower your bird.

* Hard placemats
You will want enough to encircle the base of the cage. This will catch the
excrement that will inevitably be deposited over the edge of the cage when
the bird is on top. Hard placemats can be easily wiped down, and will often
stay in place more easily than other options. You can keep them secure with
double-sided tape or glue dots if need be.

* A carrier
I cannot say enough good things about any form of a large clear plexiglass
carrier with a perch in it. Check out the "Wingabago" on the internet. These
carriers allow the bird to see all around them, which seems to help keep them
calm. It is easy to keep an eye on them, as you can see inside perfectly. The
material helps contain sound so if they do scream in the car, they won't break
any eardrums. They're easy to clean, and stand up to the beak of a U2. We
love ours, and our avian veterinarians have highly complimented the carrier.
Anything even remotely like it will work a million times better than a cat
carrier, and the perch allows the bird to feel secure as they are jostled about in
travels. Small animal carriers can work, but the plastic will not contain the
bird for very long, and the size can make it difficult for the bird to stand
straight. Holes will be chewed in no time. And lastly, never use a cardboard
box. It won't contain the bird for more than two minutes.

HOMECOMING

Once you get your bird home, it is imperative to give it time to get used to things. Keep energies low, keep things quiet, and slowly introduce them to their surroundings, and their new family. This is a great way to introduce any pet to its new home, but it is especially important with U2s, due to their heightened emotional intelligence.

If you have the bird in a cage, do not reach into the cage. You may get bitten because the bird is bound to be uncertain whether or not it is in danger from the strangers in its presence. Allow the bird its privacy, and let it feel that the cage is its safe place in amongst all of this newness in its life. U2s are incredibly sensitive and emotional creatures, and it is important that this be respected. If you force too much on them too quickly, the acclimation process will take longer. Patience is key.

During this acclimation period: keep the bird in a quiet area; do not put your hands in front of its face; it's a good idea to play soothing music; keep the television volume low; and spend time sitting near the cage quietly talking, singing and humming to the bird. If the bird is in a cage of any kind, you can cover the back and sides, and leave the front open so the bird can watch life go by, while feeling protected. If the bird has its own room, just hang out on a chair in the room. Talk to your new bird, read to it, let it get used to your presence and voice. Allow the bird come to you in its own time.

I've found that Benjamin especially mellows when I whisper to him. It has a calming effect. I can take him from a heightened state of play to hunkering down into a little snuggling ball with just a whisper. Sometimes when he's screaming, I can say in a whisper, "Let's use our inside voice," and he will quietly chatter back to me in a whisper. Honestly, hearing a U2 whisper is something you'll never forget.

If there are multiple members of family around, have each one spend quiet time near the cage. Let the bird get used to everyone on an individual basis.

Multiple faces staring into the cage at one time will make the bird extremely uncomfortable. U2s are prey animals, meaning predators hunt, kill and eat them. Humans are predators, and U2s know that. So a "trapped" bird seeing a bunch of predators staring at it, will experience an innate fear. You want to let the bird know that it is safe within your family, safe in its space, and safe in its new home.

The acclimation period can last from one day to one week or longer. It depends on the bird – its personality and its history – as well as how the bird is treated once in your home. You will know when the bird is beginning to feel comfortable based on his or her actions. Is your new bird able to sleep much? A frightened bird probably won't slip into a deep sleep. Is the bird cowering and/or shivering? Is the bird avoiding eye contact? Or staring in what appears to be fear, suspicion or distrust? Is he or she screaming a lot? Is the bird fluffing up to look bigger? Or are all of the feathers being held tightly against the body? These are all signs of a bird not yet ready to socialize with you.

You want to watch for a comfortable body posture, forward-fluffing feathers around the beak, perching on one foot, quiet cooing noises or U2 chatter, looking calmly around the room with some curiosity, and a general relaxed demeanor. If comfortable, the bird should be getting some nice deep sleep now and again. When you see these things, you will know that the bird is acclimating well. Allow the bird some time in this state of calm, before you invite it out of the cage, or try to handle it. Your patience will pay off.

During this period the bird will want to remain in the cage. But once the bird is relaxed in your home, and with the people around, it will need to be outside of the cage for at least several hours daily. Remember they are not beautiful decorations for your home. They are sentient beings, with feelings and needs to be addressed and recognized. U2s have extremely active minds, and the frustration they experience sitting in their cage can be emotionally debilitating for them.

Better than a cage, is to give them a room - one room of your house that is exclusively for your bird. It isn't a luxury all families can provide, but if you can, you will have a very happy bird. It will allow the bird to move around freely, and keep its active mind appeased 24/7. I truly believe it is the best option for a happy, well-adjusted U2. Note - it should not be an empty room. Nor an empty room with just a cage in it. It should contain a nice variety of entertainment sources.

When you do finally handle the bird for the first time, offer your arm in a fashion that shows the bird it is a steady perch - straight and strong. If they think they will fall off of it, they will not climb onto it. When they do climb on, hold still so they know you are providing a safe perch. And be prepared for their claws - they can be sharp. Best to be wearing a sleeve of some kind, rather than a bare arm. The sleeve should not be so loose-fitting that it could cause the bird to slip while on your arm.

As you and your bird become more comfortable with one another, the "steady" aspect of the arm-perch you offer becomes less of an issue. In time, you can pretty much offer them a fingertip and they'll climb on, because they trust you won't drop them.

When they climb up onto your shoulder they may use their beak to grab a hold of the fabric of your sleeve or collar to help them along the way. Sometimes Benjamin uses my hair or ear. He never bites down hard – just gets a little grip in order to steady himself as he climbs up my arm. Know this beforehand so you don't freak out and think they are trying to bite you. They use their beaks for climbing all the time.

You will be able to tell the difference between a deliberate bite, and a climbing bite. Deliberate bites are lightening fast - you can barely see them coming. Climbing bites are just part of "the process" and happen at a casual pace.

Lastly, if they do bite you, do not throw them to the ground. Being thrown down can break a leg or a wing, or damage their beak - there is no telling all of the injuries that could come of it. They generally do not bite and hang on - they bite and let go. So as calmly as you can, firmly but without shouting, tell them "No," put the bird into its cage, take care of your wound, and be more careful next time you handle the bird.

Do not hold a bite incident against them. You have the power to forgive and forget (just don't forget it as a lesson). Up your game when it comes to paying attention and reading their body language, increase your caution, but don't treat the bird differently if you can help it. Make your next visit with the bird seem as if nothing happened. It's not easy, but it's important. You are showing them that you are a reliable and steadfast caregiver, not prone to outbursts or unpredictable behavior.

The bird will more than likely test you, just like a child, to see what it can get away with, and to see what kind of person you are. Your bird is trying to figure you out. Always show them your best side.

It is rumored that there is a "honeymoon period" in the first couple of weeks with a new 'too in your home. So you may not see the "true" personality of your bird right away. They may be sweet, and become a holy terror later. We did not experience this period with Benji, as his personality has remained relatively unchanged, other than becoming more trusting over time. So I cannot speak to it, other than to pass on the theory.

HOUSING

Due to their destructive nature, implementing a U2 into daily life can be arduous. What is best for them is not always best for us. Especially if in a cage, an Umbrella Cockatoo must spend a lot of time outside of its enclosure, and should not be unsupervised when roaming around the house.

Providing proper housing is essential, and can be difficult, but is an obligation that comes with the acquisition. They need sufficient, comfortable housing for the twenty hours of each day that they are not spending supervised outside of their enclosure. It is your responsibility, and it can be a costly one. "Any old bird cage" will not suffice.

Using an aviary is better for U2s than a cage. Using a room is better than an aviary or a cage. Most cages are far too small for U2s, who need a lot of space. Can you even imagine living every single day of your life sitting in one spot? A 70 year old bird kept exclusively in a cage has spent 25,550 days – or 613,200 hours – or almost **37 million minutes** sitting in one spot.   U2s need to be able to move – to walk, run, and fly – to spread their wings and stretch their legs. Since they can't do those things while locked in a small cage, they sit on the perch becoming more and more stir crazy, their legs and wings cramping up, and they will climb the cage walls and scream until their lungs give out. Or, they will find a way to open the lock... Cockatoos are nature's escape artists.

Your U2's home should not be directly in the sun or next to a window, as the temperature fluctuations can critically harm the bird. Most say they should be placed in an area frequently used, so that the bird will feel like a part of the family. While I personally agree with the logic of this, I myself went a different route, which I will go into later.

Depending on its size, an aviary allows flight room, and can contain some flora to simulate the out-of-doors. Do your best, no matter where they live, to recreate an environment that incorporates some of the things they do in the wild: Digging in dirt, foraging for food, moving around freely, flying... If you are able to provide an aviary with flora, it is critical to make sure that the plants you put inside are not toxic. This is also essential if you let them roam freely in your home. Remember, if they can reach it, they will chew on it. You can find lists of poisonous plants on the internet, or get the information from your avian veterinarian. Seek out plants that the bird can actually eat, or inexpensive non-toxic plants that can be easily replaced. Also, expect that the soil will be tossed about – because it will. 'Toos love to dig.

You can use fake plants, as long as you understand that they will be destroyed, so it's not a good idea to spend too much money on them. Benji can disassemble and chew a tall fake tree to nothing but nubs in three days. It's why I buy them in quantity at thrift stores. He sure does enjoy taking them apart, and the ensuing mess is worth the fun they bring him. There are wires in the branches of fake trees, so once the leaves have been stripped, pull the wires from the trunk so that the bird doesn't ingest any of the wire, or get poked as he or she is working on the next branch.

If you use a standard bird cage, it should be at the very least, 4' long, 4' wide, and 5' high. This will not give them flying room, but will allow them to move around a little bit. A bare bones rule of thumb - if they can't stretch their wings fully in every direction, the cage is too small.

If they are kept in an enclosure, they will be on the perch for hours at a time, so the cage should have perches of various dimensions, or one perch with a variety of diameters, to avoid the creation of sores on their feet, as well as pain and damage to the bones and joints in their feet. **Never** use sandpaper or rough perches. They are marketed with the purpose of keeping the bird's claws filed down, but the claws don't rest on the perch – the soles of their feet do. And the soles of their feet will get torn up on a rough perch, making every second of sitting on that perch a painful ordeal.

The cage should be filled with a number of toys, hanging from the cage top, and from the sides, to keep the bird entertained while it is in there. You can buy toys, make your own, or retrofit children's toys for this purpose. Including a number of foraging toys is a great idea. There are some fascinating options available on the internet, and of course, you can build your own.

I find that many times, Benji will play with a toy for a day, and then not look at it again for months. Consequently, variety is good. I'm not saying all U2s are like Benji, but my guess is most are. And if they are, you can't put five toys in the cage and expect that to do the trick for 24/7 entertainment. You need to buy 25 (as an example), and circulate them. There may be favorites that your bird always wants around, so be sure to leave those in when rotating out the less popular.

A suggestion I would make is somewhat controversial, and apparently only works for male U2s. I call them man caves. While the man caves have been wonderful for Benjamin, it was brought to my attention that the nest idea I am bringing forth is not as suitable if you have a female bird. Having a nest available can cause their reproductive hormones to kick in. This can cause them to lay eggs. Especially in situations where the bird's nutrition is lacking in any way, they are not getting enough calcium, or if they are obese, their eggs can become bound inside them, which can prove fatal. So if you have a female bird, skip this idea.

From Forthebirdsdvm.com, in an article called "Discouraging Breeding Behavior in Pet Birds" there is applicable advice:
"Keep your bird away from dark, enclosed spaces. Most parrots are cavity nesters, which means that instead of building a nest out in the open they look for dark, enclosed spaces in which to lay their eggs. In order to stop your bird from laying eggs it is essential that she is kept away from such areas. Nest boxes should be promptly removed. Birds can be ingenious when looking for a nesting site (under a couch, behind the microwave, even in the dryer!), so it is important that she is under close supervision when out of the cage."

That said, if you were keeping your male bird in a cage or aviary, adding a man cave can be beneficial. Find a cardboard box that is at least big enough for your 'too to turn around in (and preferably move around in), cut off the top flaps, cut out a small door, and a window or two, and put it on the floor of the cage, upside down, so the doorway is on the bottom. Inside the box, place a folded towel or baby blanket, or a thin pillow such as one for a dining room or upright lawn chair. Put paper towels or newspaper on top of the box, because the bird will poo from the perch, and the poo will inevitably land on top of the box. This will allow for easy clean up – just swipe away the paper and replace it with new.

This box will be a nest to the bird. Cockatoos build nests inside of holes in trees. They don't cut out their own holes – they find those that are already there. At most, they will expand the door – as will your 'too.

Some speculate that having a nest can bring out "nesting behavior" which can include aggression. I have not experienced this at all. I found that the nest will give the bird some privacy, give them a place to store toys or chewing materials, and give them a place to go when standing on the perch becomes boring or painful. Your bird will feel some ownership of the nest, so cleaning it will probably have to be done when the bird is elsewhere, and should be done weekly. Go through the items your bird has chewed up, taking away sharp pieces of wood, and any food they've taken inside. But leave whatever you can, as it is "their stuff." Shake the blanket (outside) to remove dust and dander, then replace it in the box, and put all of their stuff back on it. **If you find that your bird takes a lot of fresh food into the nest, then it should be cleaned out daily rather than weekly.

Any room that houses a U2 should have an air filter/air purifier, and the filter should be cleaned or changed frequently. The same advice holds for the home's HVAC system – use strong filters designed for increased dust in the home, or for pet dander. The filters will have to be changed more frequently than normally suggested. Bi-monthly is a good start. Cockatoos are unique in their quantity of powdered dander. All they have to do is give themselves one good shake and it's like Pig-Pen of The Peanuts – a cloud of dander poofs off of them. Actually, I read one description on a forum which I found to be accurate – "the dust is like clapping erasers together." Showers and baths will help limit the amount of powder they drop, but it will still be an issue of note. And if you wind up with a bird who is afraid of water, like Benjamin, the dander problem will be more intense. Even on a normal basis, it can profoundly affect any individual with asthma or lung problems of any kind. It is one of the reasons many of these birds are re-homed. Their dander has created, or intensified, lung issues for people at risk.

Wherever you keep your bird, you must supply them with humidity (if needed), and unfiltered UV light to keep them healthy. They should be in 50-70% humidity, at a temperature of no less than 70F (21C). Whenever possible, they should get 10 minutes of actual sunlight a day, or at the very least 30 minutes per week, in order to maintain their Vitamin D requirement.

When it's not possible to get a sufficient amount of sunlight, the UV bulbs come into play. Vitamin D is necessary for adequate calcium absorption. Without it, among a host of other medical issues, their bones will break easily or become deformed, and eggs can bind in females.

When cold seasons make it impossible to get the bird outside, you can use UVB bulbs on a daily basis. Generally they should be replaced every six months. These are also known as "reptile bulbs," and "basking bulbs." Zoo Med and ReptiSun are two reputable manufacturers of these bulbs. Benji dislikes UVB bulbs, and often avoids them. He stares at them with some distrust. I believe it is because birds can see a spectrum of light invisible to us, and perhaps there is something in the UVB bulb's light that is disturbing to him. So whenever it's on, I play with him in his room to keep him under the tube light hanging from his ceiling. If I didn't do that, he would hide from the light. My research has not yet found an answer to why the light could be disturbing to a bird.

Do not hang the bulb anywhere near the bird, or where the bird can get to it. They could chew on it. They won't comprehend that the bulb is breakable glass, or that the cord is electrified, and that the ensuing damage could be deadly. The bulbs should not be on 24/7 – just enough to provide them a bit of UV each day when they cannot get outside to enjoy the real sun.

Sunlight coming into a room with an open window and screen can provide sufficient daily sun as well, as long as the bird is in that spot for ten minutes. But again, if in a cage, the sun should not be directly on the bird for more than ten to fifteen minutes, or the bird can overheat.

An outdoor aviary is a wonderful thing to have for your bird. You can find some for a pretty reasonable price on the internet. You can also use an outdoor dog kennel, assuming it has a closed top. Having a place where your bird can enjoy the sunshine for as long as it wants to, while also being safe from predators, is a huge bonus. The aviary should have a shady spot so your bird can escape the sun if need be.

We got an outdoor aviary for Benjamin, but he only sits in it quietly for a few minutes. Then he screams. He prefers to run freely outside, or ride on my shoulder while I slowly roam around the yard. Benji is very "anti-cage."

The majority of U2 owners have perches around their homes, and they place the bird on the perch for its time outside of the cage. I myself bought four nice big perches so I could have Benji with me in the major rooms of the house. Unfortunately, like his cage, he wanted little to do with the perches. He put up with them for awhile, but would eventually find a way to climb down off of them, or he would scream bloody murder. When he would stay on the perch for longer than five minutes, he would chew on the wood until eventually the perch was no longer able to hold him. So it wasn't an answer for us, but perches work very well for many U2s, as a way for them to hang out with their people. It's best to get one which does not have a base platform with the legs along the outside. The placement of the leg section attached to the perch floor needs to be distant enough that the bird cannot reach down from the perch floor with his beak, and grab a leg. If it can do that, it will not stay on the perch, and will use the leg to shimmy on down to the floor.

This last housing option I am going to discuss is my favorite. It has worked extremely well for us, so I am going to go into some detail.

The Room. In our home, we were lucky to have a downstairs bedroom that had a painted concrete floor instead of carpeting. We used it as an art room, so I could get paint on the floor and not freak out about it. But when we decided to get a bird, we cleared it out, put a large cage inside, and set it up for the bird's arrival.

It worked out beautifully, especially since Benjamin was the bird we got, and he loathes cages with every fiber of his being. Apparently two years in a cage too small for him was his limit. Once we got him home and let him out of his carrier, he immediately displayed his genuine distaste for cages. He would use the perches on top for sleeping. But he never went inside the small cage that came with him. And he only went into the large cage we had gotten him, a few times in his first two weeks, with the door open I should add. And then never again.

We learned over time that just because the concrete floor was a good fit, did not mean that the rest of the room was. And, over time, as lessons were learned, we made adjustments. We took down lower shelves, which Benji used to climb to the higher shelves where I kept the ipod and speakers, a small tv, dvd player, dvds, some books, some toys, etc. Don't ask how many of these things were damaged in that one shelf visit – you don't want to know.

We removed the table which he was able to climb in order to chew massive
gauges out of the wall-length window frame. The table also helped him
reach the shelves.

We had an electrician come in and move all of the outlets up to an inch below
the ceiling (not an inexpensive endeavor). We blocked the now-chewed
wooden closet doors with various items like a toy box, some cardboard
boxes, and a small rolling three-shelves-of-baskets unit filled with toys.

We eventually gave up and let him chew apart all of the baseboards. And he
did some damage to the door, created by chewing on the bottom. I should
add here that when you use cardboard boxes to block things like closet doors
or baseboards, you might be surprised to find that the damage still
occurs. You just didn't see it happen because your bird chewed through the
back of the box, revealing the luscious wood behind it. So until you move
the box, you won't even know about the fun your bird has been having behind
your back...

When we moved to a new home, we used what we learned from having
Benjamin in his own room, and we hired a firm to build a separate Benji-
specific room inside our large basement. The basement is 900 sq ft and
designed for car storage, so it is one big room.

Now, I know what you're thinking. The basement? That's not an appropriate
room for an Umbrella Cockatoo! They're supposed to be in a cage in the
middle of the home. They're supposed to be where people spend the most
time. Basements are cold, dank rooms where one stores things no longer

needed. And you would be correct to say all of those things. I've read stories about Umbrella Cockatoos being found abandoned in basements long after families have moved away, or kept there alone because the family could not handle them. It breaks my heart.

However! In our case, we had a large residence built in the basement, specifically for our bird. We call it Benji's Playhouse. This structure gives Benjamin a place to be that comforts him, allows him to do whatever he wants, whenever he wants, 24/7, and muffles sound so that he is not bothered or awakened by the lives we lead around him. Originally, it was intended to be used only as a sleeping space, as we wanted Benjamin to spend the majority of his days upstairs with us. But it turned out that he loved his playroom so much he preferred being there to being upstairs...

Benji's Playhouse is an 8'x10' room with an 8' ceiling, sound barriers in the walls, and three windows with screens – each window opens for ventilation. It has metal plates on the bottom half of each wall, no baseboards, no outlets, and in the ceiling there is a connection vent to the basement HVAC system we had installed so we could keep the basement warm enough for him. This HVAC is separate from the system supplying the upstairs living space, so can be set at its own temperature. The room has a heater in addition to the HVAC heat (so in the winter we can keep the basement at 70, and his room at 75-80), a humidifier, a Honeywell air purifier and a Rowenta Intense Pure Air XL air filter (which is fantastic). These items all serve critical purposes, and as a side bonus they help create a quiet white noise around him so he isn't bothered by the sound of the furnace, or when we vacuum upstairs, run the water, or flush the toilet. All appliances are plugged into outlets outside of the room in a space Benji cannot get to, with the cords laced through a hole in the wall. All cords are out of Benjamin's reach.

The humidifier is on a shelf in the room, along with a lamp, small purifier, and a baby monitor. The heater is outside of the room and protected by a barricade so he cannot get to it when in his play space. It is pointed into Benji's room through a small metal door that can be closed when the heater isn't on, with a grate between the front of the heater and Benji's room. The Rowenta air filter is kept inside his small "sleeping" cage. We put that small cage in his room because it provided him with a perch on which to sleep, and allowed a safe haven for a large necessary appliance – i.e. the air filter. And because the cage is placed in a corner, it provides a great space for one of Benji's caves. That particular man cave is his favorite place in the world, actually.   The only flaw is that he is hunkered down in it so often, and so rarely on a perch, that his three tail feathers take quite a beating.

Because we have taken steps to make sure he cannot destroy anything important, or be hurt by anything electrical, in this room he never hears the word no. He can chew on anything. It is all for him. It is Benjiland and he is King. And the King likes a messy room. I still clean it daily, much to his dismay. But between you and me, I have to do it - there are times when it looks like a landfill. I swear he must be having other birds over for parties, because it's hard to believe one little bird can make some of these huge messes overnight.
https://www.youtube.com/watch?v=wNYPQRlmxLE

In his room he has various man caves – six to be exact. He keeps different toys in different nests, and while he uses each one now and again, the man cave underneath his cage is the one he uses every single day, for hours upon hours (upon hours). It is his home base. His 0, 0, 0, 0 – held in eternal dibs. And no one is allowed in.

I am not permitted to take things from it. I am only allowed to toss things into it, but each item is judged as to its nest-placement-worthiness. Sometimes they are accepted (it's weird how honored I feel when that happens), and other times they are tossed out, often landing in my lap or at my feet. I should add that when I say "I am not permitted," it's not that he stops me. It's just that I can tell it annoys him, so I don't do it unless absolutely necessary.

Benji naps on the perch on top of his cage, as is normal for a U2. But he also naps underneath the cage, in his man cave. It is outfitted with a folded, thick soft blanket, and he keeps it filled with all of his favorite toys of the moment, and a generous supply of things to be chewed to bits throughout the day and night. It is also where he sits on his egg. One of the toys I gave him shortly after we got him, was an orange ping pong ball. He tries to hatch it several times every year. https://www.youtube.com/watch?v=8c3F9_rve_s

He happily spends a good 50-60% of each day in this, his favorite man cave.

There are metal floor unit shelves in the room for him to climb so he can see out the windows, and each playhouse window is lined up with an exterior window so he can see outside. He can also see outside from the perch on the cage - it is lined up so he can see through the window of the door to his playhouse, which faces a wall of windows to the side yard. It's nice that he can see outside – trees, sky, birds, horses...

However being able to see outside has its downside. For some reason, Benji hates lawnmowers and farm equipment. If he can see my husband mowing the lawn, he will scream until he can't see him anymore. I can live with that. But when the hay field next door is harvested, it is a two days of incessant screaming. Luckily it only happens twice a year. Those are loud, difficult days in our house.

The playhouse walls are lined with boxes and baskets and durable toyboxes full of toys for him. His stock of toys has grown exponentially since he first moved into Benji's Playhouse. I have watched him wander around, peek through various containers, and eventually choose a toy. I have also watched him pick up a toy and move it from one, to another container. This also happens when while cleaning, I have put a toy somewhere it did not belong... He will go to where I placed the toy, snatch it in his beak, give me a look that tells me I have done wrong, and he will put it where it is supposed to be.

Oftentimes he will walk out from one of his man caves, go directly to a specific toy and take it back to the man cave – seeming to know exactly what he wanted for that purpose, at that time, and where that item was stored. He knows what he wants. He knows what he has. He knows where things are. And he knows when things have been moved by someone other than him (that someone being me).

This playhouse provides him so much joy that it is where he always wants to be. I created a large space for him upstairs, so he could be with us throughout the day. We skipped having a dining room and instead gave the entire room to Benji, putting upside down boxes along the walls to protect the baseboards. We put one of his larger cages there so he can climb up to the top and hang out (see pic in Intro chapter). We put in a long metal shoe rack that he loves to climb and perch on, which allows him to look outside at the back yard and horse pasture. I also had a large basket of toys there for him. I say had because after two years we took the play space away. He rarely wanted to be upstairs with us, so he and I either play outside, or in the Benjiland Basement. Those are the places he wants to be.

When I took him upstairs to spend time there, he almost always screamed within fifteen minutes. He wants to go back to the place where he doesn't hear "no." He keeps himself very busy alone in his playhouse. We can hear him at all hours of the day and night, rolling his #1 favorite toy across the floor, or throwing sticks around the room. His #1 favorite toy by the way, is a 1.5 lb barbell. Weird, right?

He's played with that barbell every single day for three years. Every. Single. Day. If I put him to bed at night, and perchance the barbell isn't in his room, he will scream mercilessly. When I open the door to check on him, he either skitters down the side of his cage, runs out to his play space to get the barbell, and then takes it to his room, or he will stand on top of the cage and chatter emphatic words I don't understand, until I do understand, and I find the barbell and bring it to him. He will not relax without it nearby. At bedtime, he props it up on its side by his man cave, or rolls it into the cave to keep it safe.

Hoisting this barbell around everyday has caused him to be somewhat of a Herculean bird. He's very strong. He can pick up a can of corn and throw it off the counter. https://www.youtube.com/watch?v=xPR_fq0tUfM

He himself weighs 600 grams, or 1.3 lbs, and he can pick up that 1.5 lb barbell a good 2" off the ground and throw it at least 3". Yes indeed, he is an itty bitty Hercules.

We also set up a play space for him outside of his playhouse.

Basically about 500 sq ft of the basement is dedicated to King Benjamin. The outside play space is similar to his playhouse. Lots of toys, man caves, things to climb on, things to poop from, things to chew on, things to throw around, and things to climb inside. There are gym mats, baby mats and rugs on the floor. There are walls built of milk crates which he enjoys climbing. There are several 10' long gates (the kind meant to keep children or pets out of specific rooms, or contained in certain spaces) which he loves to climb, poop off of, walk across, sing from, scream from, and perch on. I bought him a small wooden bridge that would normally go in a garden. He has only walked across it once, and climbed on it twice to get a toy I had placed in the middle of it, but he enjoys pulling loose the small chains that serve as handrails, and flinging them around with his beak almost everyday. He does the same thing with the chains on the roundpen where we train the horses.

He has a sandbox full of sand, two water fountains - one for drinking and one for bathing, and a ball pit full of styrofoam balls, corks, jacks, and wooden nickles. https://youtu.be/qWHtx5lfECw

He has a teepee filled with hay, and a tall stepladder on which he like to perch and climb.   Some days he spends time simply sitting on top of the ladder surveying all that is his in Benjiland.

The room, which has three sections, has metal and plastic shelving he plays on, chews on, and poops from. There are large boxes all over, which he plays in and chews on, baskets of toys, instruments he (sort of) plays, as well as three open spaces for running around, throwing things, and for rolling barbells and wooden or (non-toxic) metal sticks. He also has a Barbie Dreamhouse-like thing in which I hide items, and he finds them. He climbs it like King Kong and looks in the windows and doors, where he'll find a toy, or a small baggie of seeds and/or treats. One of these days I hope to get a picture of him peering into a window, taken from the "inside" of the house.

And yes, even with all of this entertainment provided to him, he still sometimes shows signs of boredom when he and I are playing in this space. But for some reason he never seems bored alone, inside the confines of Benji's Playhouse. So weird.

To protect the few wall corners in his play area, we put up metal corner protectors. Before they were installed, Benji did take a few chunks out of the plaster. With these protectors in place, he can try all he wants, but he will not succeed in damaging the corners. In some areas, we have also used something called "raceway channels," which hold electrical cords in a metal casing. These keep electrical cords safe from prying beaks, as U2s love to chew on cords. I have read that because they do not have saliva, they can bite an electrical cord and not experience too much trauma, if any at all. But I've also read that they do have saliva, and can get shocked and burned, or perhaps even die, so... It's simply important to keep them safe from the allure of the cords. Better safe than sorry.

I think one of the best things about this arrangement goes beyond the entertainment factor, and lands smack dab in the "never say no" category. This was proven by the fact that his play space upstairs had a lot of the same fun things in it, but it also had baseboards, outlets, wood and plaster corners... So he heard the word "no." He heard it frequently, actually. I believe because of this, he was only happy there for a limited time. But downstairs, everything is designed so that Benjamin can simply act like an Umbrella Cockatoo without any human restrictions placed upon him. And there is much happiness in that, for both of us.

Another advantage to this set-up is that Benjamin is so happy in his playhouse that he rarely ever screams during the hours that he is on his own. He is happy to see me for all of my visits throughout the day, but is not particularly upset when I leave, as he has things to do. When I'm with him in his room, he seems to feel that he must entertain me. Consequently, every now and then he even requests that I leave, so he can get back to those things he wants to do. If he does carry on because I'm leaving, it ends quickly, and he goes back to playing on his own without losing an ounce of happiness. I have even had a rare day or two when I was only able to be with him for an hour, and he was just fine. Twenty to twenty one hours on his own by average, and generally not a peep of discontent.

Leaving him to his own devices in a room does mean that a certain amount of cleaning is required – I assume more so than if they're kept in a cage, but I can't say for sure. The nice thing is, Benjiland is not part of the general house space, so very few people see it. Some mornings I can go into the room and barely anything has moved. Other mornings, I can't even walk across the floor. Most mornings are something in between those two. But again, it is a self-contained mess, not visible to most who enter our home.

Benji is not crazy about my cleaning his space. He runs around trying to distract me as I pick things up and sweep the floor. He tries to get me to interact with him by bringing me toys, or snacks - a stick to throw, a grape or apple slice to share. He puts his little foot out as a request that I pick him up and put him on my shoulder. And very effectively, he asks for kisses. He stands in front of me, up on his little tippy toes, and he juts his beak up toward me as a kiss request. That one always works.

One day as I watched Benjamin in the baby monitor, he was wandering around his room, looking at all of his stuff, and talking to himself. As I watched him shuffle around, I wondered what would be the human size equivalent to his playhouse. So I did the math. As it turns out, having an 8x10 house, with some space taken up by "furniture" and "stuff," he winds up with what would be the equivalent of a human living in a 1,421 sq ft home. Once I realized that, I understood why Benji is a pretty happy bird.

He gets a lot of exercise in his room on his own. He walks around, runs around, throws things, chases his weight and wooden sticks, carries things here and there... This exercise helps keep him healthy, and takes some of the onus off of me to make sure he gets movement in his day.

Lastly I want to say that I was extremely lucky that our our life was conducive to Cockatoo ownership, both in housing and in the temperaments of our personalities. It's important that people understand this going in – getting a U2 when the stars have not aligned, or you know will fall out of alignment someday, is not a good idea, no matter how much you may want it. You must be able to keep the bird in the largest space allowable, keep it in constant toys for chewing and foraging, and must be able to give it a lot of your time – probably right up until your last day on this earth. This is not a gerbil, which has a lifespan of 3-4 years. Once in your care, your U2 will always be in your care. Always. You are adopting an extremely intelligent, hyper-active, sometimes dangerous child who will never age out.

U2 COMMUNICATION

Learning how to communicate with your bird is one of the most important things you can do for them. It is right up there with keeping them entertained. It requires a good amount of time and study to be able to do it well. Knowing what they want or need will create and maintain a strong relationship, and will help keep your bird calm and happy. Without this ability on your part, your bird will become frustrated that it is communicating with you, but with no positive results. Frustrated birds scream, have tantrums, bite people, and self-mutilate by chewing on or plucking their feathers, and chewing holes in their skin. So while it can take some time to learn, it is imperative for the health and happiness of your bird, and consequently, your own.

U2s use body posture, feather placement, and vocalizations to communicate. Their body language (posture and feather placement) comprises about 90% of their communication. Because the majority of humans rely heavily on audible language, we slip into a state of complacency when it comes to noticing body language. We generally have to teach ourselves to pay attention to their body language when interacting with our birds.

Feather placement is their primary communication method. In the case of a U2, you also have the activity of the crest. Under normal conditions, the crest is down, lying casually across their head and neck. When they're interested in something, or excited, it raises up and sometimes extends out, displaying the umbrella shape. When playing in an excited fashion, they often puff their body feathers slightly and hold their wings out just a little bit, with the crest up, as they run around or play.

They also pull out the umbrella to make themselves look bigger when feeling fear or aggression. They will puff up their body feathers as well, in dramatic form, and sometimes they will hiss and rock back and forth, I assume in a move of attempted intimidation. They may spread their wings partially, or as wide as they can. I've heard this referred to as "popcorning" - I assume because they look like a piece of popcorn, or because they appear to fluff like a container of Jiffy Pop on the stove when it bursts to expansion. I have only seen Benjamin do this once. I found a rubber severed hand at a thrift store, and bought it thinking it would make a great photo opportunity when he chewed on it. I took it into his room, and as soon as he saw it, he puffed up as big as he was able, and just stared at it. Alas, no photo op was to be had, as he never saw the hand again.

I've read different opinions on what is being expressed, but basically, when frightened but not necessarily aggressive, the U2 will stand tall and thin, and pull all of its feathers in as closely as it can. They may hiss, or simply hold their beak open, ready to bite should they decide that self-defense is necessary.

If a U2 walks or runs at you with its feathers tightly pulled in, or sometimes in the big puff, it is a move of aggression – U2 attack mode. Usually in this act, their beak will be open because they are going to bite. Note that when they run in play, it is a joyful run – often more of a fast hop or skip. When they run in aggression, they are looking directly at you, making a beeline toward you, and nine times out of ten, their feathers will be aerodynamically pulled in tightly. When this happens, it is best to get out of the way. Never kick or swat at a bird. Simply get out of the way. If possible, leave the room, and allow the bird to calm down before approaching it again.

A very happy, calm and content U2 will fluff the tiny feathers around their beak forward, and their body feathers will be in the comfortable position – not fluffed, nor flat. When extremely relaxed, they will hunch over and gently scratch their head and chin, twirl their chin feathers with their foot, or play with their feathers in another way. Benji sometimes twirls the tiny feathers on his behind, like a little girl twirling her hair.

When tired, the U2's eyes will usually slip into more of an oval or almond shape rather than its standard circle. If the bird is snuggling with a person when sleepy, the wings can sometimes fall open as they slip into deep relaxation. They do this because their muscles are 'letting go' due to their relaxed state. And they will yawn. It's really cute when they yawn. That's the nice side of a tired U2.

The other side is that they can get nippy and overly-excited. Like a small child, they can be tired and hyper-active at the same time. They go from yawning to running around the room in a flash, especially if there is a lot of energy in the room. When tired they can become clumsy and trip on things, fall from your shoulder, or just bump into their surroundings. Some get screamy. It's best if you sense that your bird is tired, or if it's past their nap time or bedtime, to leave them alone and let them get some sleep. A hyper bird can be a nippy or biting bird.

When a U2 is not feeling well, it will fluff its feathers and appear tired for hours at a time. If you see this, it's time for a visit to your avian vet, because this is not normal U2 behavior.

Then there are the vocalizations. My favorite is the chatter. It is U2-speak: a bunch of sounds that imitate human language but aren't actually words – or at least not words we can ascertain. It's wonderful to hear. They also sing, some use actual discernible human words, and they scream. They scream in joy, anger, confusion, frustration, fear, and sometimes, I swear, just to hear themselves scream.

Their scream is their laughter and their tears. Their scream is their way of saying that they need something, as well as their way of yelling at you. And their scream is their way of telling you that they love you. I once read a line that went something like, "sometimes they are just so filled with joy that they have to scream to let you know how happy they are." I thought that was really nice, and I think of it whenever Benji goes on a screaming rampage. It helps.

Once you have gotten used to the variety of screams you can often figure out which is which, noting not just circumstances and environmental factors, but also things like the sing-song quality of the happy scream, the heightened droning quality of the bored scream, and the "where are my ear plugs" loud, razor-sharp angry or frustrated scream.

As I mentioned, some of them do use human language - but not all of them. Do not buy a U2 if you are doing so because you want a talking bird. Many never talk at all - they just sing, chatter, and scream. It is not guaranteed that a U2 will speak. That said, generally those who do talk, don't do so until they are at least 2-3 years old. It is said that they must feel safe in their environment in order to talk, and it can take years before they are able to speak well enough for anyone to understand the words.

An interesting fact is that U2s will often make requests of you in gradations. First, they may ask softly. If there is no response, they will ramp it up a notch. If they still get no response, they will take it to the next level – until they reach the need to scream, nip or a bite. For instance, when Benji wants to be on my shoulder, he will offer his foot to me by raising it off the ground. If I were to ignore this request, he might start following me around, with a lot of chatter – that is request #2. If I ignore that, he would probably start in with a scream - request #3.

Think of it in terms of making a request of a child. First request is light - "Honey, please pick up your toys." If ignored, you move on to something like adding a bit more tone in the request, usually coupled with the word "now." If still ignored, some anger or frustration creeps in... And this goes on until the final measure of a time out or grounding. It's the same thing with a U2. But in the U2 scenario, we are the children...

A more painful communication is the U2 bite. They bite when they are provoked, tired, overstressed, ill or injured, as well as when they are over-stimulatd or playful.

Of the six or seven bites I have received from Benjamin in our time together, all were accidents (while playing) except two. The first exception was in the first two months we had him. I took him outside on my shoulder, and it began to rain. Benji hates being sprayed with water - with a passion. He let me know he wanted to go inside. I walked too slowly for his taste, because he was getting wet, which made him angry. As we were heading back to the house, he swooped in to bite my face. Luckily for me it happened just as I was reaching up to move hair from my eyes. So instead of face, he got finger. And he got it good. The second exception was the last resort in trying to tell me it was time for him to go to bed. He had told me with chatter. He had told me with screams. But due to the annual time change, I didn't think it was bedtime yet, and missed his clues. I did not leave his room. So he bit my ear. Hard. And I left his room to go to the ER.

Sometimes U2s will add dance moves to the screams. Benji has one particular dance he does all the time. We call it the Benji Shuffle. For this dance, he hunkers down a bit, and then shuffles to the right three or four steps. Often while shuffling, he wiggles his wings and screams. On the last step in the shuffle, he leans far to the right and kicks his left leg out, like a Rockette. He then repeats the same thing, but to the left. He will do this over and over again for anywhere from three seconds to three minutes. Sometimes it includes the scream, and sometimes it's just the dance. I have learned that he is telling me a few things with this dance, and I have to figure out which one it is. 1) I'm bored and want to do something else but don't know what yet. 2) I don't want to be in this location (used when he is anywhere except Benjiland). 3) It's time for me to go to bed. And 4) I'm feeling very happy right now.

Cockatoos do a nightly "shout out" to "their flock." Just as the sun goes down, they scream a few times to let the other Cockatoos out there know where they are, and that they are safe. I have read that they also do a morning shout out, but it is not something that I have experienced. The 'shout out' can last for only a few screams, or can go on as long as a few minutes. It's loud, because its purpose is to travel long distances to communicate to U2s all around them.

Speaking of which, I'd like to take this opportunity to spell out how loud U2s can be, just so you won't be surprised. Sound is measured in decibels (db). Normal human conversation is generally 50-60db. Anything over 70db over a long period of time can damage your hearing. Anything over 120db can cause immediate damage. 125db is considered "weaponized sound."

A Cockatoo's scream is in the 120-130db range. It is weaponized sound. It is 10-20db *over* the average human pain threshold for sound, so will feel like weaponized sound. Other things in that same range – a chainsaw, a jet engine, and a rock concert. In 1972 the Guinness *Book of World Records* listed Deep Purple's concert at London's Rainbow Theatre as the loudest on record, at 117db. Concerts are now a bit louder, with Led Zeppelin and AC/DC coming in as high as 130db. But for the sake of this paragraph and point, a screaming U2 would be louder than Deep Purple performing ***in your home***. A little *Hush*, or *Smoke on the Water* anyone?

Ok, so I want to make sure this is clear. The shrieking scream of an Umbrella Cockatoo is ear-splittingly, mind-numbingly, earth-shatteringly loud. There is no escape - unless you leave the house and drive away. There is nothing enjoyable about it. Rather, it can make you want to slam your head into a wall (seriously, I've thought about it). And it is ongoing - for as long as they choose to scream. Unlike a dog, they won't stop just because you say "quiet," or, "stop that." There is very little, if anything, you can do to stop a Cockatoo from screaming if it wants to scream.

Most fascinatingly, it is a strangely grating noise that could take a Buddhist Monk from peaceful prayer to brutal violence in a nanosecond. It triggers something animalistic in your brain that will surprise you. I have to wonder if there is something about the sound that is an evolutionary characteristic designed to scare away predators, because it really does trigger the strong desire to run away from it – for as long and as far as your legs will carry you. It is imperative, before you adopt a U2, to know this. Actually, you shouldn't just know it, you should *understand* it. You are inviting into your home for probably the rest of your life, a being that will, daily, make an ongoing noise which will cause you to cringe and reflexively cover your ears.

The sound of a U2 scream is unique among the Cockatoo specie. Most Cockatoos have an at least somewhat enjoyable scream. But the U2 does not. There is a 2005 film called The Descent, wherein a woman's family is killed in a car crash, shattering her life, her love, and her soul. A year later her friends invite her on a cave exploration holiday in hopes of easing her pain. Most of her friends are killed in the cave by inhuman underground dwellers. In the sequel, she is taken back into the cave by authorities who believe she killed all of her friends in that cave. Don't worry, there's a point here...

At the end of the second movie, these creatures, who cannot see but have a heightened sesnse of hearing, are bearing down on the one remaining police woman in the cave. To allow the authority to leave the cave alive and go home to her young daughter, the lead lets out a scream to call all of the cavedwellers to her. She lets loose with a scream that holds in it all of the pain, anger, and misery she has felt over the loss of her family, and the deaths of her friends at the hands of these creatures. The destruction of her life, her child, her husband, her best friend... The misery of spending the preceding 356 days waking each day trying to hang on to a life she doesn't even want to lead without her loved ones by her side. The emptiness, frustration, sadness and anger... It's all expressed in that one resounding, heart-wrenching scream.

The point? Dollars to donuts her voice coach for that scream was an Umbrella Cockatoo.

If you, or anyone in your family, has temper issues, this is **not** the bird for you. The noise alone can trigger a temper tantrum immediately upon hearing it. They rarely "ramp up" to the loud scream. It's just abruptly there. You can be sitting in silence only to have it suddenly slam into your ear like a sledgehammer. It is only slightly less loud, and therefore only slightly less surprising and painful to eardrums, than a gunshot. If a temper – yours or anyone else's – is a part of your time on this earth, this is a bird that will make life more difficult, stressful, perhaps even emotionally painful for you and/or your family.

Summarized, if an ill-temper has any role in your days, this is a bird that will suffer in your life, and will eventually have to be re-homed. This is a bird that is only a good match for the most patient or hard-of-hearing.

Lastly on the screaming, your best bet is to try to preemptively stop it – figure out the body language of your 'too, and know when it's about to scream. Immediately distract the bird, and there is a chance that you might be able to quell that scream into silence before it even comes out. I do this with Benji frequently.

I still let him scream daily, just because a) I know sometimes he enjoys doing it, b) I can take the opportunity to clean or get something done that I know will make him scream anyway, and c) it's good for his lungs. Plus, I never want to stifle a scream of joy. So if that's going to take place, I just cover my ears, sit back and let it happen. But often, his screams when we spend time together are these weird, "I don't know what I want to do next" screams, or the "you're not doing what I want" screams. When I see that he's about to belt one out, I get him interested in a toy, give him cuddles, massage his neck, talk to him, kiss him on the head. https://youtu.be/HlpbCpDrDnM

These usually work. When they don't, I just wait it out. If it lasts too long, in an act of sheer desperation, I dance. When I dance, it often stuns him into silence. Apparently even he can't believe someone can dance that badly...

Okay, that's out of the way. Now let's look at some of the quieter aspects of their communication. I'd consider the beak clicking also a vocalization, though it does not come from their vocal organ (the syrinx). The beak clicking is a chewing action, where the upper and lower beak join up over and over. It can sound similar to the "chattering" sound we make with our teeth when we are cold. Now and again the bird performs another sound - something similar to a clicker (as is used in clicker training), where the lower beak "clicks" off of the upper. It's a bit strange, if I'm to be honest. I've only seen Benji do it the second way twice in the years we've had him. Both times, it looked and sounded different from the "chewing" method of clicking. Instead, it felt almost as if he was trying to train me to do something. (click, click "Who's a good Amy?" click, click)

The beak clicking or clacking tells its story in speed and volume. When rapid and loud, it means "leave me alone." It can be a pre-bite warning, or just a simple, "Go away now, I'm done with you." When done slowly, or somewhat rapidly but quietly, it's generally a greeting, or outflow of affection. It takes time to discern the difference. I find it's best to look at the situation and factors involved to ascertain the meaning. I compare it to when my husband and I had a 5 ft long Giant Green Iguana: Iguanas use jaw clicking and head bobs as communication. There is one particular head bob that can mean both, "Hi'ya! So good to see you!" and also, "I am two seconds from ripping off your face." This commonly-used head bob movement had two diametrically opposed meanings, and it was up to us to know which she was saying. It can be the same with the U2 beak clicks. So I repeat, consider the situation, and what you know about your bird, before you make assumptions on what is being communicated by the rapid clacks.

Lastly there is the beak grinding. This is a sound created by pressing the upper and lower sections of beak together, and grinding them side to side, or front to back. It is a sign of contentment, and can often be heard as the bird is preparing to go to sleep. This movement also serves to trim the beak.

Talking birds developed the ability to mimic sounds as a way to fool predators, which is probably why a caged bird will use this skill. A caged bird can feel like prey, and is using its evolutionary wiles to deal with its situation. Eventually domestic birds (not "domesticated," but those living in domestic situations) turned that ability into more of a manipulation than a protective behavior. Because they are such incredibly social creatures, they *need* to interact with the living beings around them.

In a domestic environment, they are around humans, so they use human sounds to "fit in." They desire a close relationship with their person, and therefore use the human's own words in order to do so. It is also why they bark and meow in homes that include cats and dogs.

I was talking with one U2 owner whose bird clearly and beautifully says the words, "I love you" to her. She told me it's necessary for him to say that often, because 99% of the time he's a "total dick." It is his saving grace. It is how he manipulates his situation. He's a "dick," she gets angry, he says "I love you,"' and she forgives him. As I write that out, I can see how that mirrors some human relationships...

There are experts who are realizing that birds can learn context in language, and apply it to decide which word or phrase to use under the circumstances. For instance, they know to say, "Hi" or "How are you?" when you enter a room. This is generally because these are the words they hear their people using when others enter a room, or they are the words their people use with the birds themselves. Talking birds will use the same language they hear – English, Arabic, Japanese, whatever they hear... complete with proper inflections and intonation. I'm quite certain my Benji knows a little Spanish.

It has been found in recent years that some small birds are using linguistic rules in their communication that were formerly considered exclusively used by humans. They found that the Japanese Great Tit, a bird closely related to the North American Chickadee, uses grammatical rules in its communication, similar to our phonological syntax. For example, suffixes and prefixes are sounds that have no meaning on their own, but create meaning when attached to a word. The JGTs use this same rule with their calls, which makes one call mean something different than the original meaning. For instance, by adding a certain sound to the end of a call, they can transmit the original meaning of the call, while also adding information that there is a predator nearby.

Spelled out, let's say the original call is "aaa," and means "come on over." Add a "b" to it to make it "aaa-b," and it tells the bird, "come on over, but watch out for the predator I spotted." If they put that same inflection in front of the call, say "b-aaa," it has no meaning. This is comparable to the word "sudden" made into "suddenly." If we were to put the "ly" on the beginning of the word, it would have no meaning - lysudden is not a word.

As we learn these things, I don't think it will be too much further down the road when we find that animals can communicate with us on something very similar to "our level." For them, ours is simply in another language.

Up until recently, there was no belief from anyone other than people living with talking birds, that a bird could use words in context. Bird owners would excitedly tell others how their bird requested a specific food right before dinnertime, or asked if a particular family member was going to visit soon. And anyone listening would smile sweetly while silently thinking, "Oh my goodness, she has gone off the deep end..." It has long been believed that while birds can mimic words, any semblance of context or understanding is merely coincidental.

And I have to say, I don't know why it would be so unbelievable. They're extremely intelligent, can form words, they pay attention to how we use words, so why is it not believed that they can then use those words in context? You hear about people learning another language simply from watching television. Our birds are learning from watching us. Again, I don't purport to be an expert, but I think everyone who has ever said that birds don't know what they're saying should go watch this video of a U2 named Chief. He is arguing with his person, who apparently left him in his cage for awhile after arriving home. Watch the video and pay close attention to what the bird is saying, as well as the body language. It will change your idea of talking bird communication forever. Here is what I, and others, have deciphered, in transcript form:

https://www.youtube.com/watch?v=1ijiGPrl3fM

Eric: What?

Chief: I was <f-bomb> laughin'. I was right there.

Eric: You're mad because we didn't get you right away?

Chief: I really did expect you both to stop.

Eric: Why are you so mad?

(Chief looks at Eric as if he can't believe that Eric even has to ask that question.)

Chief: I'm your <f-bomb> fluffy white brother. I am not a bother.

('I am not a bother' is slowly and clearly enunciated, as if he's trying to get the point across, with an emphasis on "not.")

Eric: Because we left you out...

Chief: <indiscernable but the word 'you' is there.>

Eric: We just left you in the cage...

Chief: You <f-bomb> stabbed me in the back! (Lots of wing emphasis)

Eric: We just left you in the cage for a second.

Chief: It was FOREVER! (Massive body language with that line)

Eric: Why are you so mad?

Chief: It was snowing out!

Eric: It was just a second.

Chief: It was snowing out there. (Points to "out there" with his right wing, and it appears there could be a dusting of snow on the ground, visible through the window)

Eric: We just went to the bedroom for one second.

Chief: (looks at Eric with skepticism) <says two things that are indecipherable>

Eric: I'm sorry. What do you want me to say? I'm sorry.

(At this point, Chief's beak feathers move forward, slightly covering his beak, which is a sign of happiness in a U2. He is softening.)

Chief: I plucked it out, but that's worse.

Eric: So, are you gonna calm down now so we can go to bed? Hmm?

(Chief looks at him with beak feathers forward, but head held high as he is still undecided if the matter is closed...)

Eric: I said I'm sorry. Is that good enough?

(More silence from Chief)

Eric: I won't leave you on top of your cage when we go to the bedroom.

(Chief has heard what he wanted to hear, and his tone becomes friendlier.)

Chief: I hope you don't.

Eric: Ok, deal.

Chief: Ok, deal.

When you watch this video, you can clearly see that this is a bird having a conversation. This is a bird using words and phrases in context. Eric cannot understand what Chief is saying at the time, so the dialogue is pretty one-sided, but it is obvious that Chief knows what point he wants to make. He knows what is being said because the words he uses are all germane to the situation. His feathers come forward to cover his beak, and his intonations and body language all become more toned down, less exaggerated, once the apology is made. It's truly a most fascinating video and look into what can transpire between a bird and a human.

Yes, you can compare it to how you can hear voices in white noise. Perhaps it is similar to hearing what you want to hear in 'too speak. But even if you disagree with the translation, you cannot deny the body language, the intonation, the facial expressions, the emotions, and the potential amazing use of human language used by this bird, to get his points across and carry on this conversation. It is unique, fascinating, and really causes one to wonder just how far their communication can go if given the chance.

Alex, the parrot who worked with Irene Pepperberg for years, could identify and name 50 different objects - numbers, materials, and shapes. Alex proved that he was able to grasp the concepts, "bigger", "smaller," "same," and "different." He was learning "over" and "under" just before he sadly passed away. He could recognize quantities up to six.

Animals communicate with people everyday. They can be the most simple behaviors such as a dog doing the pee-pee dance at the door for instance, or a cat rubbing its cheeks on you to mark you as their own.

Our cat saunters from her litterbox after she pees, but she bolts and runs away after she leaves a more solid deposit - her way of telling us to go clean the box right away. Our horses tell us if they want a fly mask, or fly spray, or a blanket. They tell us when their hay bowl is empty, or if they would prefer to be in a different pasture than the one we have open for them. All you have to do is "listen."

I put a new fly mask on one of our horses, and she didn't like it - she wanted the one she usually wore, which was hanging on a stall door. So she told me by making a particular sound, called a sentry breath, which they do when they are concerned about something. When she had my attention, she touched her usual mask with her nose. Her way of saying, "Get this mask off of me - I want *my* mask!" As soon as she had her usual mask on, she trotted off happily to the hay bowl. Horses cannot form words, but she clearly communicated with me.

Many members of the parrot family have a leg up on other animals, because they can form words. We don't even bat an eye when one is taught to ride a tiny bicycle, but so many people question the bird's ability to use a word or phrase correctly. That's strange to me.

Nowhere near the conversation with Chief, Benjamin has a few examples of using words and phrases in context:

When I leave his room temporarily, I usually say, "I'll be right back." He then knows that I'll only be gone for a minute. If I do not return quickly enough, he will yell, "Be right back!" as if to remind me of my promise.

Benji likes standing on my arm and being catapulted up and down – he bounces and flaps his wings. It's as close as he can come to flying. One night as we were doing this, I had to end the activity because his claws were painfully digging into my skin. As I brought my arm down, I said, "Ok, that's all mama's arm can take - we have to stop now." He climbed off my arm, and said, "Did that hurt you?" I responded, "Yes, it did, thank you for asking."

While perched on my shoulder looking outside he said, "What's that?" I replied, "That's rain." He said, "Oh. Rain. Pretty."

Once while he was talking, I laughed, and he clearly said, "Don't laugh at that." https://www.youtube.com/watch?v=gnHMaAJEALo at the 3:20 mark - I did not catch that until I was watching the video later. I still haven't figured out what I was not supposed to laugh at though...

We play a game using a long box which is lying on its side. He runs into the box, and I roll his barbell in so he can roll it out and back to me. Before I roll it in, I always say, "Are you ready?" because I don't want the barbell to bump into him. It usually stops at the edge of the box entrance, but I fear hitting him if it goes in further and he's not paying attention. Sometimes I say it as he's standing outside the box watching me, and it is his cue to run into the box. In between rolls, he climbed up on a shelving unit and pooped. So I stood up and got a paper towel. He had climbed down and was waiting in the box for me to roll the barbell, while I was wiping up his poo. He waited for me patiently for a few seconds, and then I heard a tiny voice inside the box say, "Ready!" He did not say "Are you ready?" as I do. He simply used, "Ready."

As we were wrapping things up one night, I was sweeping the play space, and he was running around near me. I said, "Where is your weight?" because I had to have it to put back in his room for bedtime. He walked into the box, I heard the sound of things being shuffled around, and then he rolled it out of the box and said, "Here!"

Twice I have accidentally bumped him with my hand, only to have him once say, "Ouch, I just got hurt," and the other time, "You hurt me." Both broke my heart and elicited extreme apologies from me, but also made me laugh heartily.

There have been numerous conversations I have had with Benjamin where I thought, "Wow, I have to tell Howy about that." But then I forget to tell him, and I forget to write them down, so they are quickly lost in the murkiness that is my aging gray matter.

It took me awhile to learn exactly what Benjamin was saying to me in his communications. Benji is still quite new to speaking, so his words are somewhat garbled. Add that U2s do not mimic human language well – you can sometimes understand the words they are using, other times the words are there but indiscernible, and other times they're just chattering. Birds don't have vocal cords. Their sounds are made through vibrations in their chest. Sometimes Benji can say things I can understand, while other times I can figure out what he's saying by watching it on video. But most often I respond only to the situation and his inflection, as the words are unknowable at that moment.

After some time, he and I both got to know each other so well that I often knew what he was going to do before he did it – sort of like husbands and wives who finish each other's sentences. I'm still guessing at a few things, even after years with him. I think it's important to note that while there are general communication methods that all U2s use, there are also things that will be specific to your bird.

There were so many excellent responses to the question, "Do parrots know what they're saying?" on Quora.com. People with years of experience living with parrots responded to the question with their examples of how they know their birds are speaking in context. I would highly suggest anyone interested give it a read.

There is a wonderful story on the website http://exoticdirect.co.uk, by Donna Schwarz, from October 2016. She tells a story of talking with Paula, an owner of an American Grey parrot: Like many Greys, if Rachel does not get what she wants, she insists. Her favorite food, corn on the cob, is prepared in the microwave. When the microwave pings, she often calls out, "Corn!" If corn is not forthcoming, she will sing in an operatic voice, "Cooooorrrrnn."

Paula returned one day from the office and, as usual, greeted her Grey, "Hi, how are you Rachel?" The bird replied, "Incarcerated." Her owner told Donna that she never taught Rachel that word, but assumes Rachel heard it used in conversation.

When the question, 'do parrots speak in context' was asked on the reddit.com forum, there were some spectacular responses. For instance, poster peony33 wrote, "Charlie knows 'no.' I swear I thought he repeated it, until 3 days in a row he said 'no' when I asked him to step up, and said 'no' when I told him to come here. He never ever says it out of context which leads me to believe he actually knows what the hell he's talking about."

Another response: Poster WhisperingWisps wrote, "Luna was playing on my laptop. I was going to give her a little tap to encourage her to move a bit (she was covering an important part of my screen!) but before I touched her she said, 'no.' So I stop with my finger in the air and pull my hand back. Then she said 'Good girl!' And that my friends is how you train your human..."

And from someone who was apparently trying to get his or her bird's attention (no author name given), "One day I was kind of annoying my GCC, and he turned a glaring eye towards me, and with an annoyed voice said, 'WHAT?' I was taken aback and apologized for annoying him."

Garwoodwould adds to the conversation: "There hadn't been an infant in our house for, probably, ten years. One day, our friends brought their newborn over and, naturally, the baby started crying. You should have seen the parents' faces when the bird said, 'You want a bottle?'"

Punkin_Pie tells the story of how her bird can use sounds to tell her what it wants. "My bird says 'pretty bird' when she sees or hears birds outside. He makes a spitting sound when I brush my teeth. He mimics the sound of a spray bottle used in cleaning, but repeats it when I'm washing dishes or cleaning the counters. He makes a water sound when I turn on the faucet or when he wants a bath and the faucet hasn't yet been turned on."

TheyCallMeFreckles posted, "My greenwing loves to sit outside with me when it's nice out. He will regularly yell 'hi' or 'hello' when he sees people walking by. Again, something he probably picked up from me since I'm friendly to our neighbors. Our house sits on the corner and once someone startled him (he probably had his head buried in his breakfast) and called hello to him first. He jolted and said, 'Oh!' very clearly before saying hello back. I thought it was funny because that's something I usually say if he drops a toy or I knock something over. That was the first time I had actually heard him say it but he apparently felt that was an instance where something unexpected happened and the response should be 'oh!'"

Eptitude writes: "My African Grey has recognized my fiance by name for a long time. If she wants him, she'll specifically say, 'Connor' pretty much persistently until he reacts. She also knows that he taught her how to say 'boop' and that he laughs at her and sometimes treats her when she says it. Therefore, it's now very common to sit down with her and the conversation to go along the lines of:
Arya: "Connor?" Connor: "Yes, Arya?" Arya: "BOOP" And then she laughs maniacally.

And two more examples... jbatty74 tells of her thoughtful bird. "I was in the bathroom reorganizing my toiletries when all of a sudden I fell. Followed with a huge crashing sound of the toiletries falling. Sammy without hesitation came over and said, 'Are you ok?' I almost died. It was so cute and caring."

And ishey writes: "OK – here's context for you: CAG: 'What cha doing?' My son: 'Making a ham sandwich.' CAG: 'oh.' My son: 'Birds can't have ham. It's bad for you.' CAG: 'What! Dammit."

Lastly, I think a poster named not_sure1220 makes an excellent point, which I have experienced so many, many times... She writes, "I think it's hard to get a video, because the times we do converse with our parrots are short and random times. Rigby, my GCC, has spoken in context many times, and when I try to get it on video he decides all he wants to do is chew on my phone."

She adds, "For example, when it's bedtime, Rigby will fly upstairs and look down on my boyfriend and me. If we just sit there and act like we don't know what he wants, he'll say, 'Night, night,' and then he'll fly up to his sleeping cage and wait for us to come up and tuck him in. The best evidence I have that Rigby knows what he's saying is when he sees us doing something new to him. The first time he saw me brushing my teeth he said, 'What are you doing?' Then he did it the first time he saw me unloading groceries and when he saw my boyfriend shaving for the first time. He doesn't say it every time. It's always when we're doing something new or strange. I have a lot of other stories about how Rigby communicates with us, but I won't drone on about those. Parrots are extremely intelligent and while there aren't tons of videos out there, us parrot owners know our feathered friends aren't just mimicking. They are fully communicating with us. :-)"

DIET

There is a lot of advice out there on what and how to feed your bird. Keeping a U2 on the *best* diet for them is very similar to keeping a person on the best diet for them -- it should be easier than it is.

The bowl in the picture underneath the chapter heading is one of many I gave to Benji in the early days. I would serve him a bowl like that daily. He would eat the apple slice. The rest would be ignored, or strewn about the room, sometimes with distaste, other times with a bit of glee.

Basically, a U2's diet should be as natural as possible. Like all birds in the wild, they spend much of their time foraging for food. They eat nuts, seeds, grain, and can crack though coconuts with some ease. Although, if you watch Cockatoos in videos in Australia, you will also see them sort through garbage bins in residential neighborhoods, and eat whatever foodstuffs they find.

They say that for domestic U2s, seeds should be a small part of what they consume - they need fruits and vegetables, and pelleted food. The pellets contain a blend of grain, seeds, fruits, vegetables, vitamins and minerals. As it is with people, it is with 'toos – not all of them like fruits and vegetables, and will be very choosy about which ones they will eat. You should feed them a large variety over time to see what they will consume, and what they will toss to the side. The selections they toss aside should be considered again later, as once thrown away does not mean the bird won't eat that fruit or vegetable a month or six later.

Some sources say that a good 80% of their diet should be pelleted food. Others skip pelleted food altogether. If you go the pelleted route, which is what I chose, I advise that you buy a few small bags of different pelleted food so you can experiment. Some will be eaten with abandon, while others will be completely ignored. Don't buy large amounts until you are certain which ones they will eat. You don't want to be saddled down with a 20 lb bag of a food your bird won't touch (as I was).

There are many references on the internet to the proper Cockatoo diet, which can make it confusing. Everyone has an opinion, so all you can do is sort through and decide what you believe. Some say use dried fruit, while others say only fresh. Some say never feed them dairy products as U2s are lactose intolerant, while others include cottage cheese, yogurt and grated cheese on their list of things to feed your bird. Some say feed them only small amounts of fruits, while others say fruits can be a mainstay of the diet. It goes on and on. The bottom line is that you need to find that "happy place" diet for your bird, through experimentation. It takes some time, and it will probably be frustrating.

You'll also want to consider your bird's lifestyle. If they're in a cage for a large part of the day, just sitting, you don't want to load them down with fattening sunflower seeds and peanuts. (You also don't want that bird to be an Umbrella Cockatoo, because they do not do well just sitting in a cage all day...) You'll want more vegetables in the mix than anything else, to keep their weight down. If they're extremely active, then they can pretty much eat whatever they want and not put on unhealthy pounds. Well, grams, actually – unhealthy grams.

Some domestic U2s wind up being raised on a high seed diet, and then it's difficult to get them to eat the right foods when they are in your care. They only want seeds. They say when trying to transition them, never use the "eat what I put in front of you or starve" approach. It is rumored that the bird will starve itself to prove a point. Benji was on a seed-only diet when I got him, and I had to transition him to pellets, fruits and vegetables. He fought me every step of the way for quite awhile, and I became extremely stressed over it. But eventually I found a pellet food he would eat, and gradually he opened himself up to a few fruits and vegetables. To get him there though, I had to use some desperate methods...

I started eating meals with him, allowing him to eat off of my plate. We did not "share" food, but I made a section on my plate with bits of my food cut up for him. You see, Benji loves company while he eats. He loves to stand near me, on one leg, hold the food he's eating in his little foot, and chat with me while he eats. I adore this activity. He looks so cute as he nibbles away on a food while keeping me entertained with a running commentary of Cockatoo chatter, often with his mouth full. He actually made a yummy sound when he tried a piece of pizza. Turning it in his foot while looking at it, he went, "Mmmmm..."

At first I assumed that letting Benji eat alone was wise, as it gave him something to do to pass the time while I wasn't around. But I was wrong. Whether human or bird, company is a plus when breaking bread. I've read that many 'toos will eat best when they are allowed to eat with the family. I saw a video of one couple who set a plate at their table for their bird, who joins them for every meal, sitting in a child's highchair.

In this process of eating with Benji, he would try different things off of my plate. It is the activity that finally opened his mind to eating things other than seeds. He'd grab a french fry, a piece of egg roll, a bite of a sandwich... off my plate. (I did not use any foods that have a toxic aspect to them, such as onions, garlic, and avocado, which are all harmful to birds.) Then I started creating plates of fruits and veggies along with my usual items. So he'd have a bite of french toast, and then try a strawberry, or piece of banana. He'd have a bite of grilled cheese, followed by a floret of broccoli. He tried a bit of green pepper on a piece of pizza. He also snagged an entire chicken leg from my plate before I'd gotten it myself, tore off the meat, broke the bone and ate the marrow. I admit, I was a little creeped out by that. But it was such a relief that he was finally eating things other than seeds, and for the first time, I began to feel as though he wouldn't drop dead from lack of nutrition.

Unfortunately it was very difficult to keep a variety of fresh fruits and veggies around for him - I learned that just because he ate a piece of mango yesterday did not mean that he would eat it again today. I had to learn to enjoy the same foods, otherwise I had a lot going to waste...

As I worked on the transition, I tried baby foods (he'd not touch them), dried fruits (bananas, coconut and pineapples were enjoyed), home-baked treats using bird-specific recipes found on the internet (he didn't eat any of them), low or no-sodium canned veggies (corn, peas, and a variety of legumes were all popular), many varieties of organic granola bars (hit and miss), and of course we ran through the gamut of every fresh fruit and vegetable on every bird food list on the 'net. Sugar snap peas, fresh green beans, corn on the cob, apples, grapes, bananas and pears were the only ones that were eaten now and again. Everything else was thrown to the side each and every time I put them in his food dish. Anything fresh, by the way, should be thrown away after a couple of hours of sitting in their bowl. And if the fresh items left any juice or fleshy bits on the pellets in the bowl, those too should be thrown away, or outside to the wild birds (who won't let it sit around for more than a few seconds). It's not a bad idea to keep fresh fruits and veggies in their own bowl.

Since he is such a fussy eater, our saving grace has been the smoothie. https://youtu.be/XEx2Uk3r5aU

I make a smoothie for myself almost every morning. They include some combination of: spinach, kale, strawberries, blueberries, mango, peaches, acorn squash, zucchini, yellow squash, orange, lemon, lime, raspberries, blackberries, elderberries, carrot, and apple. I add water, beet powder, Greek yogurt, flaxseed, chia seeds, and hemp hearts. I add a splash of sugar-free flavored gelatin powder to decide the final flavor. Okay wait, I should be honest. I put in more than a splash - more like 1/4 to 1/3 of a packet. Without it, the vegetables make it taste pretty horrible. With it, the smoothie is delicious, and packed with things I would never eat otherwise.

And as it turns out, it is the same for Benjamin. Other than the apple, he will rarely eat anything in the listed ingredients. However, he will often drink smoothie by the beakful. Once he started drinking those with me, I felt much better about his nutritional intake. I also made (by accident - I forgot to put in the butter) a butter-free banana nut muffin, and he enjoyed it very much. It was actually surprisingly good, so I now make them often, and Benji always gets to share with me.

I found that his curiosity usually gets the best of him, and he would almost habitually eat something if he saw me eat it first. It of course does not help with items I won't eat - raw Brussels sprouts or his pellets for example. But nine times out of ten, if I eat something and he's watching, he will come over and request a sample bite. It's been a useful trait of his, I must say.

As I mentioned, I learned that just because Benji ate something once or twice, does not mean I should stock it as a staple. He would eat apples for a week, and then refuse them for a month. Pretty much the same scenario for everything except grapes. And grapes are apparently so full of natural sugar that they should only be fed once a week, according to our veterinarian.

Nuts are good for U2s. To Benjamin, all nuts are deemed inedible and tossed out of his bowl, except pecans, walnuts, peanuts, and almonds – but he will only eat almonds in the shell. If I give him an almond not in the shell, he throws it away. Go figure.

When they eat pelleted food, they do so dry, as well as wet. They enjoy dunking their pellets in their drinking water. Consequently, their water bowl often needs to be cleaned out and the water changed a few times a day, because when they dunk the pellets, or leave them in the water to soak, bits of pellet can break off into the bowl and will begin to smell unpleasant. Apparently, if you feed them dried fruits and vegetables, they may also dunk those into their water bowl to hydrate them.

Another option I found helpful was to find something Benji liked, and add things he needs to it. For instance, he enjoys peanut butter. He loves to eat it straight from the jar (he has his own jar). To use this to my nutritional advantage, I create tiny peanut butter sandwiches for him, using either a 12 grain bread, or an oatmeal bread - it barely matters in his case as the bread is rarely eaten, but merely a transport vehicle for the peanut butter concoction. In the peanut butter I mix in chia seeds, flaxseed, cooked acorn squash, and/or cooked sweet potato. Now and again I use banana. It almost always works. If I get cocky and add too much of the nutritious stuff, he tosses the sandwich to the side, and I learn. The peanut butter must be there in good quantity, or it will not be eaten.

Grooming note here – when they eat messy foods, like peanut butter, their beaks should be wiped off with a paper towel. When doing so, be careful because sometimes they chomp down on the towel and your finger is incidentally bitten. Benji likes me to wipe the outside of his beak, and then he takes the paper towel into his beak, squishes it up and then chews on it to clean out the interior of his beak. Or, he flings it in the air and runs away.

Food suggestions

Some basic fruits:
Mango
Apple
Orange (not in great quantity, large amounts of citrus can cause iron overload, as Vit C increases the amount of iron supplied by other foods)
Banana
Pineapple
Papaya
Coconut
Apricot
Pear
Grapes
Peaches
Blackberries
Blueberries
Raspberries

Vegetables – fresh, canned or frozen with no added salt. Most should be served cooked, but not hot:
Corn
Peas (spring, sugar snap)
Broccoli
Sweet potato
Squash
Zucchini
Bell pepper (can be uncooked)
Green beans (can be uncooked)

Celery stalk and leaves (uncooked, and there are great nutrients in the leaves)
Carrots (can be uncooked)
Dark leafy greens (can be uncooked)
Asparagus
Beets
Bean and alfalfa sprouts

Misc:
Cooked rice, cereal, pasta, cheese and meat (including eggs) can make up 10% of your bird's diet. Benji enjoys salmon, which appears on a few food lists. Any raw meat must be fresh. Benji has grabbed bites of fresh raw hamburger and has relished them. I will share that his poo smells a bit worse the next day.

Beans such as Pinto, Garbanzo, Black, etc., are enjoyed greatly. They must be cooked. Raw they can be toxic, due to a lectin called phytohaemagglutinins. If using canned beans they do not need to be cooked (as they are already) but the juice should be rinsed off thoroughly. Beans are a good source of protein.

While nuts are popular and healthy in small quantities, there is a risk of aflatoxin contamination with peanuts, so some owners do not serve those. Walnuts in the shell, unless you are certain of their freshness, should be checked before being served, as they tend to rot inside the shell more often than other nuts. Inside the shell, the moisture content is around 33%, which attracts mold and speeds decay. Walnuts outside of the shell have a mere 13% moisture content, so they last longer. Moldy nuts can cause an infection, creating lesions in the lungs of birds. Most birds enjoy getting the nut out of the shell, so shelled nuts make foraging more fun – again, just make sure they are fresh. Birds do not have a great sense of smell, so they may not notice if a nut has gone bad.

Some people hang trees of Brussels sprouts out for their birds to nibble on. Some put whole fruits and vegetables out for their birds, while others slice them up. Again, experimentation is key.

Foods U2s should never be fed:
Avocados have a toxin called persin, which is poison to a bird's digestive system.

Onions irritate the lining of the mouth and esophagus, and can burn the bird's crop. This can cause ulcers, rupture red blood cells and cause anemia.

Garlic contains allicin, which can cause anemia in a bird. Anemia is a decreased capacity of the blood to carry oxygen.

Pits from cherries, peaches, apples, pears, apricots and plums, all contain cyanide, and even in the tiniest amounts can kill your bird very quickly. The meats of the fruit are fine, but not the seeds. Never the seeds. The leaves of cherry trees, maple trees, and a few others, metabolize cyanide in the wilting process, so keep your bird away from these when outside.

Chocolate cannot be given to birds. Even a tiny amount of chocolate can kill your bird due to an alkaloid called theobromine. Birds cannot metabolize this alkaloid, and it can cause vomiting, diarrhea, seizures, and death. Chocolate also contains caffeine, which is toxic to birds. Caffeine can cause increased heart rate, and potentially cardiac arrest.

Birds need fresh water everyday. The bowl should be wiped down daily, and water always clean. The water in the bowl should be deep enough that they can drink, while shallow enough that they can retrieve the pellets they drop into it.

When U2s eat, the food is often chewed up, and kept inside the bird's crop. The crop is a space in their esophagus which holds a small pouch, located above the chest cavity. The food is stored there, to be ingested at a later, more convenient time. Benjamin will quickly eat something whilst playing (dash around, nibble food, dash around...), and then later in a time of rest, he slides one of his toes into his beak to retrieve what he had taken in earlier. I usually see this when he has a crop full of chewed pellets, and then takes a big drink of water. Sometimes a slimy slurry of pellet bits and water will spill out (usually onto me), which is, frankly, a little bit gross. But most is swallowed or remains inside his beak.

The crop allows birds in the wild to take in more than they can eat at the moment, then fly to a safe place to enjoy the meal. It is also a storage place for parents to hold food they later feed to their young ones.

ENTERTAINING YOUR U2

The best way to have a happy U2 is to KEEP THE BIRD BUSY. There is a reason why solitary confinement is used as an ultimate punishment in prisons. People go crazy in there with nothing to do, left only to play inside their own minds. In the case of U2s who are kept in an empty cage all of the time, their active minds suffer greatly. The capacity for boredom relies heavily on intelligence, and U2s possess intelligence in spades. When bored or frustrated, they scream relentlessly, and pluck their feathers until the feathers will no longer grow back, sometimes even digging holes into their own skin – known as self-mutilation. It is similar to the self-harm manner of "cutting" for humans. If your bird is doing these things, there is a need, or are needs, not being met. Figure it out. Experiment. More than likely, it's going to be one or more of the following: Freedom to move, your time, or items to keep them busy.

I get a kick out of coming up with ways to entertain Benjamin. It took me awhile to ascertain what made good toys, and what did not. Benjamin had to teach me. I'd say a good 50% of his favorite toys are not ones I'd chosen, but things he found around our house on his own. Items I'd not have considered, he found to be fun toys.

I started gathering items before we got him, by purchasing parrot toys which hang in the cage. Since Benji didn't use his cage, those were not worth the expense. Even outside of the cage, they didn't interest him. I surfed the internet for more bird toys, and tried to come up with ways to make them work for Benjamin. Didn't have a lot of luck, and wasted a lot of money. Toys like the "boing" which provide a bouncy rope for the bird to hang onto, he never bothered with at all. I think because he cannot fly, he didn't want to risk hanging onto something so unstable.

I hit thrift stores and started buying children's toys, like Legos, Lincoln Logs, bags of Army men, matchbox cars, stuffed animals, plastic farm animals, cheerleading pom pons, a tiny plastic tea set, a xylophone, a bag of "super-balls," and even a desktop basketball game. In the spirit of experimentation, I just grabbed anything I thought might interest him.

I put about half of the toys in a box and set it on the floor of Benji's room. He sorted through the box, pulled a few items out, played with them briefly, grabbed a tiny horse in his beak and placed it in my brother's lap (he adores my brother), and then climbed into the box. Once in there he picked up each item and quickly hoisted them all out of the box like a tiny white maelstrom. When he was done, he was just a bird sitting inside an empty box in the middle of mayhem. And he loved it.

The next morning, I found that the box had been overturned, with an entryway chewed out, and Benji was inside with a few of the toys. He had made his first man cave, and a trend was born.

I looked for other items that were right there in our house, which could provide entertainment. Organic packing peanuts, bubblewrap, cardboard oatmeal containers, egg cartons, empty and washed out plastic bottles, empty water bottles, a roll of toilet paper... he loved them all. I would put a nut, some black oil sunflower seeds or pellets of food into small plastic bottles with lids, and hide them around his room. When he found them, he would work the caps off, hold the bottle in his beak, and lean his head back so the treasure inside would slide into his beak - like shotgunning a beer. Over the years, he has had more fun with mere household items than with bird-specific toys. https://youtu.be/I6FlGxNNFkE

I should add that there will be some purists who do not believe it is safe to give the birds "just anything," and will feel negatively about toys like styrofoam, bubble wrap, and plastic bottles that aren't brand new. I understand and respect that. But I have experienced no problems with these items, and Benjamin has been over the moon for them. A box of 50 styrofoam balls provided Benji with more fun that I have ever seen him have in one sitting. But then I rode on bicycle handlebars as a kid, and still eat raw cookie dough to this day, so...

I make various climbable structures available to Benjamin - mostly shelving units, his wall of milk crates, and a ladder. https://youtu.be/0v6BIkLmtQ4

I had gotten a few 12 oz spray bottles to use for Benji's showers. Since he hated showers, he would attack the bottle as I tried to spritz him. One day I accidentally left the bottle on the ground, and Benji played with it – for hours. At first he played with it angrily, to show it how much he hated it. But after awhile, he was obviously having fun. He chewed on it, hoisted it in the air, threw it around the room, and while holding it in his beak he pushed it around on the floor, going back and forth and over and under and around. He would purposefully get it wedged under or between things so that he had to work to get it out. He loves to problem-solve. So while it did not help in the shower department, the bottle made a toy that entertained Mr. B for a very long time.

I learned when Benji got into one of our closets that he enjoys chewing on unpainted ceramics, which were in a bag on the closet floor. Also, by happenstance, I learned that Benji *loves* toothbrushes.

He sits on his perch, holds the toothbrush in his foot, and rubs his beak with the bristles (he loves beak rubs). He runs it over his back feathers in a move unmatched by any yoga master, chews on the handle, and pulls out the bristles with his beak. That said, you shouldn't give them used toothbrushes unless they have been thoroughly cleaned. Human saliva has gram-negative bacteria, which can be harmful to birds.

You should also never let your bird play with used cat toys. Cats have pasteurella bacteria in their saliva, which is deadly to birds. (This is also why, if they are ever bitten by a cat you should get them to a vet immediately, even if you don't see a puncture.)

Plastic capsules, also known as acorns, are a great item. You can buy them in many sizes, pop the cap off, put items inside – pellets, nuts, small toys – and then re-cap. The bird will roll them around, throw them around, and pry off the lid to capture the treasure inside. I like to fill them at the end of our day together, and hide them around his room. The next morning I can see which ones he found, and which ones he has opened. Note that if you hide food in any, you have to make sure that they don't stay hidden too long...

Another fun idea is to fill zipper snack-sized plastic baggies with pellets, seeds, nuts, or toys, and seal them. Leave them around for the bird to find. Benji loves to rip through the bag to get at what's inside. He holds the bag in his little foot, squishes it into different shapes, chews on different areas, and shows glee when he gets his beak on a treat. Actually, anything in a bag is a joy to Benjamin. Bags alone are a delight. He loves to pull things out of bags, put things in bags, climb into bags – plastic or paper. Bags have a high entertainment value. Although, any bag handles could catch the bird, so those should be cut.

A tossable toy Benji loves is a roll of masking tape. He hurls these rolls all over the room, running and chasing them to hurl them yet again – over and over. No roll of tape is safe when Benji is around. I finally had to buy him his own. I came home with a plastic shopping bag filled with ten rolls of masking tape, and set the bag down on the floor of his room. He ran over to peer inside. When he saw that the bag contained not just one, but many rolls of tape, he began dancing around the room and chattering at me in a very excited manner. Then he pulled them out one by one and threw them around.

I have accidentally left partial rolls of paper towels in Benji's room enough to know that he revels in tearing them apart. Almost every roll I forget in there at night has been ripped apart and strewn about his room when I see him in the morning. He also chews on the bare cardboard roll, so I give him those when I've used the last towel in a roll. A roll of toilet paper brings the same amount of joy as a roll of paper towels - and costs less. Or at least, it did when I started writing this book. Pandemic pricing makes both paper towels and toilet paper more expensive than fancy bird toys on a per minute entertainment cost basis.

And of course, his barbell. He gets a charge from rolling it, throwing it, and propping it up on its side to then knock it over.

Before the barbell, there was wood. I had placed a piece of firewood in his room, hoping he would chew on that instead of the baseboards. While he did not really chew on it, he would in fact chomp down on it with his beak to get a grip on it, and then push and throw it around. It was not a small piece of wood... It had to weigh three pounds easily. And he'd push it around the room for hours each day. He got so much joy from that piece of wood... I wrapped a string around it at one point, and he would climb onto my arm, use the string to lift it, and I would raise my arm while he held on to the string, picking the wood up a foot or two off the floor.

As much as he enjoyed this, I put an end to that activity due to the lacerations his claws put in my arms, even when covered.

I finally had to take the wood away because he would play with it to the point of exhaustion, and then get clumsy with it. I feared it would land on his foot, so I took it one day and did not bring it back. Eventually he stopped looking for it. Luckily, he had the barbell obsession to fill the gap. The barbell was not a toy I had given him. It is one of the toys he simply took when he saw it.

Bear in mind the Cockatoo creed: What's mine is mine. What's yours is mine. If you put it down it's mine. If you touch it it's mine. If I see it it's mine. If you give it to me, I don't want it.

In that vein... One day I slipped a wooden stick under Benji's cage, into his nest. He threw it back out. I slid it in again, telling him I had gotten it especially for him so he could work his beak down. He tossed it out again. I tried one more time, putting it on the opposite side of his man cave. And again, it was removed. I said, "Okay, never mind then. I guess you don't want it." I put it outside of his reach. He popped out, grabbed it, and took it into his cave. The Cockatoo Creed.

An amusing thing I learned as a form of entertainment is, ironically, sweeping up the things he'd chewed up overnight, and putting them into a bag. He absolutely adores going into the bag to pull everything out. He sets some items aside in a pile, throws others, and kicks others out of the bag with his feet. My husband says he cannot believe my patience, to clean and then let him mess up like that. I, on the other hand, think, "Hey, I just kept him happily entertained for twenty minutes!"

I guess what I'm trying to say here is, other than avoiding toxic heavy metals (lead and zinc), toxic paint, sharp items, and anything with tiny parts, keep your mind open as to what can constitute a bird toy. You probably have many things the bird will enjoy playing with and/or destroying.

The longer you have the bird, the more desperate you will become to find things they will enjoy, and games you can play as you spend time together. I think PETA Asia explains why better than I can. From their website:

"Driven mad by boredom and loneliness, caged birds often become aggressive, neurotic, and self-destructive. They pull out their own feathers, mutilate their skin, incessantly bob their heads, pace back and forth, peck over and over again at cage bars, and shake or even collapse from anxiety."

If you find yourself running out of ideas, watch videos of the Cockatoos known to be kept by loving people: Harley, Gotcha, Max, Pebble, Onnie, and others. Look around for the scattered playthings as you watch whatever crazy antics are going on in the video. It could trigger good ideas for you and your bird.

One of my favorite things to do is reading to him before bedtime. He would snuggle up directly in my lap, or wrapped up in a blanket. But once I had to start using my reading glasses I had to cut back, since B loves to pull glasses off of people.

It is suggested that one way to keep a Cockatoo from becoming bored is to teach them tricks, or give them puzzles to solve. In 2014 a Goffins Cockatoo set a new standard for bird intelligence. From the article, Smart Birds: Cockatoos Solve a Complex Five-Step Puzzle: *"Think you have a smart parrot? That may be, but a Goffin's Cockatoo has recently set a new standard by which bird – and indeed animal – intelligence will be measured. Pipin, as the avian genius is known, demonstrated a skill previously known to exist only in chimpanzees. Using sequential problem solving abilities, Pipin (and, after a time, several of his "lab partners") figured out how to open 5 different locks – each of which jammed the next lock, and each requiring a different physical maneuver – in order to obtain a treat. Mastering the task, which took nearly 2 hours, required the bird to solve problems, remember what he learned and apply it to a different task, and focus on a distant reward...and, I assume, to have patience!*

The Experiment
The fascinating research into Psittacine intelligence was conducted at the University of Vienna, and published in the journal PLoS ONE (8(7): e68979;doi: 10.1371/journal.pone.oo68979; 7/13). Ten Goffin's Cockatoos were presented with a box containing a treat. The door to the box was transparent, so that the birds could see the treat (a nut) within, and was secured by 5 locks.

Lock number 1 had to be opened before the cockatoos could get to lock number 2, which had to be opened in order to gain access to lock number 3, and so on. Opening each lock required a different physical action – removing a pin, screw and bolt, turning a wheel and shifting a latch.

Without prior training, Pipin opened the box in less than 2 hours. The article stressed the speed of his problem solving, which of course is impressive. But I'm equally surprised by the fact that he could keep at a problem for such a long time. As anyone who has tried to train parrots (or toddlers!) knows, their attention spans are relatively short (or so I thought...maybe birds and

2-year-old children have been tricking me all along!).

Five other "less-cerebrally-gifted" but still quite intelligent Goffin's Cockatoos solved the puzzle after watching Pipin perform or following exposure to each lock individually.

Researchers Make the Test More Difficult

Sequential problem solving requires a parrot or person to remember and then apply what has been learned, and to work for a distant reward. In order to test these and related abilities, the University of Vienna researchers scrambled the locks, so that number 3 was first in line, followed by number 5, etc. Once a cockatoo had mastered a lock, it rarely became confused if the lock's place in the puzzle was changed. And locks that were disabled by the researchers (left unlocked) were given a quick glance and then ignored."

Music has been proven, time and again, to be enjoyed by U2s. All animals can appreciate music actually, and it can affect their mood as it does with humans. I play music for Benjamin everyday. I try anything that has spa, relaxation, meditation, drums, or yoga in the title. He adores dancing to drums. Listening to music with Benji has expanded my musical appreciation greatly. Weirdly, I found that he really loves Gregorian chants, and dislikes solo violin.

When we first got Benjamin, I used ocean waves to put him to bed. They'd play for about an hour after I'd turned off his lights. It always mellowed him and signaled to him that it was bedtime. So as soon as the ocean waves began, he'd climb up onto his perch, pull a foot up, and go to bed. Generally, I play mellow "waking" music in the morning, more active music during the day, and then mellow spa/relaxation music at night.

Lastly, in the entertainment realm, for the U2s who are able to fly, there are flying leashes you can use to allow your bird to get some exercise outside. I'd recommend the ones that found a way to eliminate the sudden pull that can happen when the bird reaches the maximum height allowed by the leash. You don't want your bird lurching in flight.

U2 BEHAVIOR

Umbrella Cockatoos are shockingly affectionate, extremely intelligent, highly social, and wildly destructive.

While some sources do not agree, the majority say that they mate for life, spending much time together as a couple. After one mate dies, the survivor often does not take another mate, and can fall into a deep depression. In domestic situations, they create strong bonds with their owner(s). These birds crave affection and closeness. Snuggling is a top priority when with their people, as well as concentrated attention. I disagree with the few experts who say that you should never cuddle with them. The difficulty comes when people cannot provide enough time for the bird. That is when the screaming begins. That is when the self-mutilation begins. They are consistently needy.

Some birds become protective of their owners. Many say it is because the bird sees their person as their mate, which can happen around sexual maturation at five years of age. When this happens, the bird can become jealous of anyone it sees as a threat to the relationship or to time with its person. Some speculate that this confusion is caused simply by hormones, while others say it is because of actions on the part of the owner, such as petting the bird under the wings, or on its back. They say that these are areas normally only touched by mates. As part of the mating ritual, the two birds scratch one another around the tail and head, which is believed to improve bonding.

I have to admit to learning these "petting rules" long after we got Benji, and have always felt free to pet him under his wings - not his core, just the underside of his wings. I have not "scratched" these areas - only soft pets. He adores it. It has not led to any problems, nor does he view my husband as competition. He is quite smitten with my husband. So... I dunno. So far so good. I can only hope we don't run into problems in the future.

When two birds pair up, they will leave the flock to reproduce. They will have a clutch of eggs which will contain two to three eggs. Both will share in the responsibility of incubating the eggs. Incubation takes thirty days.

Two months after we got him, Benjamin rolled an orange ping pong ball into his nest, and began sitting on it for hours every day. I don't know how long it lasted, and then one day the ping pong ball was back in a pile of toys. I guess he decided it wasn't going to hatch, and he was done. He does this several times a year. https://youtu.be/OFNf1KUQu_A

He has also done this with an egg from a plastic 'matching recognition set' I found at a thrift store. Stored in a plastic egg carton, each plastic egg breaks in half with a matching shape on both sides – it is a toy created to help kids match shapes. Benji breaks them open, but doesn't try to match them - he just throws them around the room. When he isn't breaking them open, he sits on one as a whole egg and tries to hatch it, alongside his orange ping pong ball. It's always a very mellow time, as he takes the task very seriously. He will leave for small amounts of time to play and snuggle with me, but then he goes right back to sitting on the egg(s). https://youtu.be/8c3F9_rve_s

The only downside is that during "egg time" he screams a lot when he's away from the egg. He willingly and happily comes out to his play space to hang out with me, but he's often off-kilter and screamy. Once back in his room, and in the vicinity of his egg(s), he's much better.

Something that makes Umbrella Cockatoos a bit different from other birds is a "selective breeding" practice that takes place in the wild. While they lay two to three eggs, they only raise one chick. Usually it is the first one to hatch, but if there is any deformity in the chick, they will only care for the second hatchling, or the third if there is anything wrong with the second. It is a harsh reality of nature, but is put into place because the young require so much time and attention that the parents cannot handle more than one. While most baby birds fly at two weeks, it is three months before a baby U2 can fly. They are extremely dependent upon their parents for absolutely everything until then. Once the baby can fly, the three birds leave the nest and go back to join their flock.

I've seen mention in some U2 advice that it's best to keep them off the floor. It is believed that if on the floor, they will always go after toes. Benji has indeed gone after my toes, I will admit, but it's pretty rare. Maybe six times in three years, and that's being generous. In the early days it was prompted by the action of my sweeping his room - which back then he hated due to his fear of the broom. Actually I think he was mostly going after the broom, but sometimes got my foot instead. When he got over that fear, no more toe attacks while I was sweeping.

If it's best to keep them in a manner similar to what they have in the wild - which it is - you have to look at U2s in the wild. There, they do spend time in trees, but also much time is spent on the ground, or on flat structures such as rooftops, as they forage for food. So to keep them off the ground is asking them to not do something it is in their nature to do. Also, if they aren't on the ground, that means they are mostly on perches. Too much time on a perch can cause problems with the bones and joints in their feet. It can cause abrasions on their feet, and can bring about an infection known as "bumblefoot."

I read that it is not a good idea to train your bird to only go to the bathroom in certain locations, unless they have constant access to the locations. It is physically damaging for them to retain their excrement. Their bodies and digestive systems work to metabolize food and eliminate their waste quickly, as required by their flight capabilities. It is a design by nature to keep them as light as possible as consistently as possible. Training them to "hold it in" may work well for you, but it could eventually rupture their colon.

They say larger birds don't poop as often as smaller, but I have to say the Benji poops constantly. If the waste is particularly wet, it splats when it hits the floor, and bits shoot all over. Consider this in your cage placement.

They preen themselves to remove dust and dirt, and also to align their feathers. Often, post-preen, they will fluff their feathers and shake, to be rid of any dirt or powder they loosened in the preening process. When a bird bonds with its person, it will preen them as well. While adorable, the discomfort comes when they try to remove anything that does not appear to belong there, in reality or only in their opinion. Tattoos, warts, moles, freckles, scabs, hairbands, earrings, piercings, buttons or snaps on your clothing... all are in danger of attempted removal.

They chew. You know that. I know that. Anyone who has researched them for even five minutes knows that.

They chew on anything made of wood, plastic, fabric, foam, leather...

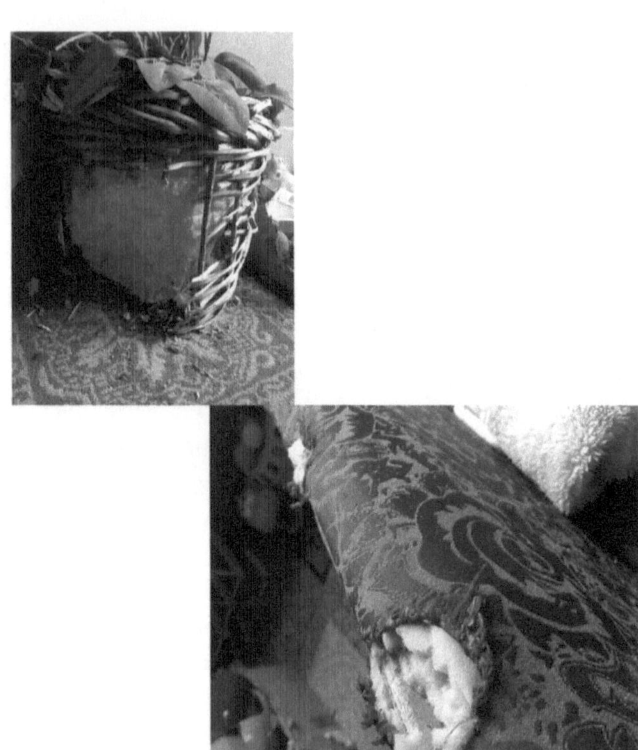

They chew on chairs, walls, and rugs.

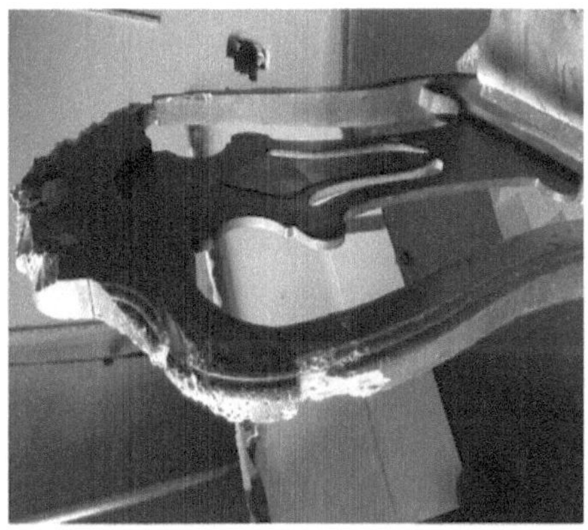

And what they chew off, needs to be cleaned up...

And the last two items: they shiver when they are cold, when they are afraid, and in extreme happiness and excitement. Also, while I have not found any clear reference to this in my research, there is something Howy and I call Benji's mucus ball, which is this little white ball he produces in his mouth when he wants to clean out his beak. It just suddenly appears, seems to be a pretty solid little mass, and he rolls it around and around inside his beak, and on either side of his tongue. He usually brings his mucus ball out after he's had a peanut butter sandwich. I have no idea if this thing is stored in his crop when not in use, or if it's something created when needed, then swallowed... No idea. But I do know that it never leaves his beak. On some forums people have talked about this, saying that their bird seems to bring it out when they relax - say, before bedtime. I am still seeking an explanation.

It seemed to take quite awhile before Benjamin was able to really trust me. We all have to remember when we adopt a bird, that it has probably lived

with a number of people before they came to us. This means that they have
had a great number of experiences on which they are basing us, and which
play a part in their personality. It will take awhile before they know who *we*
are, and what to expect from us. We were told that Benjamin prefers men
over women, so I had that going against me. I also ran into situations such as
his always acting as though I were going to kick him whenever I walked by,
so he would react by dodging my feet and snapping at them before running
away. And he would violently attack the broom each time I tried to sweep
his room. He would jump onto the head of the broom, wrap himself around
the pole, and bite down, hard, over and over again. If I left the broom alone,
standing against the wall, it would be clearly damaged while sitting there, or
be on the floor with more chew marks. It took a year for those behaviors to
vanish.

Bear in mind that every bird is different. They may all look almost the same,
but their personalities can vary greatly. As do their talents and tolerances.
Some are great with strangers, some are not. Some are too unpredictable to
take into public, while others thrive on it. Some will play happily on the
floor while others will spend every second looking for trouble. And some wi
231A2a33333333333333333aaaaaaaaaaaaaaaaaaaaaaaaaaaaaaaaaaaaaaaaaaaaaa
ll take over your computer... Benjamin just typed that word/sentence, from
the space before the number 2 to the last a. I tried to do some work on this
while he was busy doing other things. He didn't like that. Or he knew I was
thinking of him when I typed "others will spend every second looking for
trouble." But I think primarily, he was telling me to move on – my point was
made. So, that said, these are variables to the life you will have with your
bird. Like people, each one has its own unique personality.

I had the idea that when I got a U2, it would sit and play in its cage or on a
perch while I was doing other things - hence our purchase of three big cages
and four nice perches. I thought the bird would ride on my shoulder while I
did housework. It would go to the office with me and sit quietly in a cage
while I worked. None of that happened. And it was up to me to make our
life together work for both of us, and not remain stuck in some ideal-for-me
dreamworld, trying to force my ideas on Benjamin. It took time and
experimentation to figure things out, and it was entirely up to me to adapt.
Years later I'm still learning new things. So while it is fantastic to have a
base of knowledge before you get your bird, know that you will always be

learning.

CARE AND MAINTENANCE

There is not a lot of maintenance to caring for a U2. They are a hearty bird, and if given proper nutrition, exercise and attention, you probably won't experience much in the way of health issues.

If you see a lasting decrease in appetite, lackluster feathers, or notice a change in their feces, or in their behavior, you should take them to the vet. Prey animals are stoic creatures, and they do not show obvious signs of pain or weakness. They know if they are seen as weak or sick, they will be singled out by predators. Because it is innate to them to cover their illnesses, it is up to their caretakers to notice any subtle signs, and see that the bird is cared for by a vet when needed.

There are photographs on the internet which can show you what healthy and unhealthy feces look like. This would be a good place to note that if your bird eats any foods that may contain coloring, their feces may temporarily come out colored - so don't panic if their poo is bright pink (or green or purple...).

The most common problems faced are parasites, intestinal inflammation, crop inflammation, respiratory problems, and prolapses of various internal organs.

Just to be safe, you should also know that there is one illness that is not common, but is in fact contagious to humans, called psittacosis. It is a bacterium. In birds it causes inflamed eyes, difficulty breathing, watery droppings and green urates. In humans, it causes headache, muscle aches, dry cough, fever and chills. In mild cases, the symptoms last around three weeks. In more intense cases, it can result in death.

Generally, Cockatoos are very clean birds. They preen their feathers daily. But if you have a need to control the bird's powder above and beyond their own preening, the bird should be showered or bathed with warm (not hot) water, no soap, and in a warm room. In the wild, they take showers in the rain and/or bathe in puddles. If your bird does not have access to rain or a bath, you can put them in the shower on a perch, using a light spray of shower water, or spritz them with a spray bottle. It is best to dry them in the sun whenever possible. You can gently towel dry them, and some will withstand being blow dried on a light setting.

If you use a small bath tub, the water should not be deeper than 2" or there is risk that the bird could drown. They need just enough water to splash around.

I've seen so many videos of birds taking showers and baths and *loving* it, but my little Benjamin wants almost nothing at all to do with water. My attempting to give him a shower brings about a very angry, agitated, and sometimes aggressive little boy. I've read on forums that this can be a result of someone spraying the bird in a disciplinary or angry fashion. I can't say if that's true or not. Whatever the reason, Benji hates water sprayed on him, nor will he sit in water. Even getting caught in a light rain while outside with him on my shoulder, will bring about a potential face bite in anger. He may think rain is pretty, but he doesn't want it touching him. Our vet told us that as long as he was in good humidity, the lack of showers or baths would not harm him.

Luckily, Benjamin keeps himself very clean, always smells fresh, and the only thing I have to worry about is keeping his feet and beak clean, and doing a monthly gentle smoothing of his feathers with a damp washcloth. Three years in, I got a four-tier shallow bowl fountain for him, and he did begin taking ocassional "baths," in which he would stand on the edge of a bowl and throw water around with his beak, with some of it landing on his back and wings. (And the rest flying all over the walls and floor.)

There are a few things you will need to stay on top of: Claw length, beak length, and opening feather sheaths. I do not recommend filing the beak or claws yourself until you've had the bird for a long time. Even then, I'd only suggest doing the claws, if your bird will allow it. *Beak filing should absolutely be left to the professionals.* That said, if the bird has enough wood items to chew on, it generally won't need its beak filed.

Chewing on wood and other items helps keep a U2's beak trim. If they aren't getting enough to chew on, the beak will grow to an unhealthy length and must be trimmed by an avian vet. Do not take your bird to a vet you do not trust, for this task. Take the bird in for a few basic appointments with your vet first, to see how well they handle your bird, before you let them perform this delicate procedure. The beak tip is extremely sensitive. A good vet will do the trimming with a dremel tool, and will take frequent breaks to cool the beak down. The contact of the spinning wheel on the beak creates heat in a short amount of time, so keep your eye on this while your vet is working, and make sure they take frequent cool-down breaks, or cool the beak with water in the process. You do not want any beak burns or unnecessary pain for your pet. Some vets use a slower dremel tool, which will not require cooling breaks. That said, it is also not a good idea to let the beak get too long before having it trimmed. The longer the beak, the longer it will take to file down, and the more chance there is for a potential burn. If the vet uses the slower tool, it will take even more time if the beak is longer.

A happy healthy bird is a chewing bird. If your bird isn't chewing on things, there could be something wrong, so consider it something to watch. If it continues, it's time for a visit to the vet.

As to the feathers, each feather comes in as a tiny bud popping up through their skin. As it grows, the feather itself will be inside a sheath, along with blood to feed its development. These are called blood feathers. Blood feathers completely freaked me out at first. I knew that if one were broken, Benji could bleed to death, and it took me awhile to get over that fear.

Basically, the feather sheath is kind of like a cocktail straw. If it were to be broken while blood is retained, the blood would pour out of the "straw" as if it were a faucet connected to the bird's blood supply, and the bird could bleed to death. Birds cannot tolerate much blood loss, so death could happen rapidly.

The remedy is a simple one, but in those first months of ownership, I did not think I was capable of doing what needed to be done, which terrified me. You have to pull the remaining feather section out of the bird, using a tweezing device. Once the "straw" is out, the skin will close and the bleeding will stop with a bit of cornstarch, and pressure on the wound. If you cannot pull it yourself, you must find a way to stop the blood flow, using a binding clip or something similar to hold the sheath closed, and then get your bird to the vet asap.

One of Benji's feathers broke a few months into ownership. Luckily it was a very small feather, but I didn't know at the time that it made a difference in the outcome. I slathered what remained of the feather with corn starch, which made the itty bitty spot of blood at the tip congeal. I got an emergency appointment with our vet, and rushed over there. He plucked out the tiny feather with a chuckle, and explained to me that it's really only the large wing feathers, and the large head feathers on the U2s, that can cause fatal blood loss. Lesson learned.

In regard to these sheaths, on a normal basis, the U2 will gently chew each sheath open, to reveal a beautiful feather. However, there are feathers the bird cannot reach on its own, and it's up to you to open them. It is a task usually done by lifemates or flockmates, so unless your bird has a mate, it will fall to you. You simply squash the portion of the sheath that contains no blood, gently between your fingers. You can also use your fingernails - always gently.

Never get too close to the blood line. The area for about ¼ of an inch up from the blood is very sensitive. Benjamin only had to scream in pain once when I got too close to the blood line for me to never ever get that close again.

If your bird suffers no joint or muscle ailments and its movement is unencumbered, the only feathers that the bird cannot reach itself are on its head and neck. Sometimes the feathers coming in right in the middle top of the back are also unreachable, so you may have to get those as well. Keep an eye on feathers as they come in, and if you see one has gotten long but has not been touched by your bird, then you know it's being left for you. If left for too long into the growth process, the sheath will become very hard, and pretty much impossible to remove.

Two things of import: 1) Only do this task when the bird is calm. One simple twitch from the bird could transform a sheath removal into a feather removal. And 2) Only open feathers you can see. As a sheathed feather, they feel the same whether they have blood in them or not. Consequently, if you work on a feather you only feel, but do not see, you could accidentally pinch the blood-filled portion, which would be a problem, as mentioned previously. The tiny feathers on their cheeks are some of the most difficult to get, as they seem to hide behind one another when you try to work on them.

Your bird's cage, aviary, or room, should be kept as clean as possible. And they will hate it. U2s are very territorial as a rule, and they don't like people messing with their stuff. Our vet recommends using water with just a touch of bleach to wipe down surfaces. I was told that you should not be able to smell the bleach.

When cleaning a cage, the suggested practice is daily cleaning of food and water bowls, and dusting off perches and cage bars. I myself do not dry dust anything in his room, as it just re-distributes the powder. I always use a wet paper towel.

Any deposited bird droppings should be cleaned up as often as possible. Getting to them quickly makes them easier to clean, as it can stick like glue to surfaces if left to dry. When that happens, I've found a paint scraper works well. Perches and toys should be cleaned weekly to bi-weekly, and the entire cage should be cleaned monthly.

It is good advice to not "reward" your bird for screaming. They can become like the rebellious child who breaks the rules just to get his or her parents to pay attention. Anything other than ignoring the screaming, is a reward to the bird. Walking up to it, yelling at it, whatever you do, is seen as an interaction by the bird. As a consequence, the next time it wants attention, it will scream. It is suggested, and I use this method myself with Benjamin when he is in his room and I'm upstairs, that you ignore the screaming, and as soon as they've been quiet for at least five seconds, you can go to them. It teaches them that quiet, not noise, will bring the attention they seek. The only time I break from this practice is if Benji is performing his "alarm" scream, which consists of loud rapid shots of noise. Then, I check on him right away, as he is telling me something is wrong.

In the case of their screaming while you are already paying attention, you can of course try to quell the screams with pets or toys. You are there playing with them, so it's not your attention they are seeking. Simply distract them. If several attempts at distraction don't work, then go away, which tells them you have your limits, and they have just exceeded them.

A facet of the flying mechanism in birds is that they have extremely sensitive lungs. Consequently they cannot handle certain elements in the air, such as heated non-stick cookware, candles not made of soy, air fresheners, cigarette smoke, perfumes, etc. I admit to wearing perfumes some days, but I do not refresh them before seeing Benjamin. I have seen no visible reactions or negative results to my wearing a light perfume. I have seen a reaction to one of my hand lotions - he tries to lick it off. It smells like berries. That said, lotions can be transferred to the bird's feathers, so it's best not to use them right before handling your bird.

Umbrella Cockatoos should not be left alone with children or babies. Because they are emotionally needy, they develop jealousy easily, and are often rumored to be jealous of babies and small children. Others see small kids as playthings. These viewpoints could lead to a potential bite. They also have very strong claws, and they can easily draw blood in a vulnerable little person (as well as adults).

If you are able, keeping two U2s can be better for them than keeping just one. It makes great sense, though please note that a U2 should not be kept in the same cage with a smaller (non-U2) bird. But a pair of 'toos *who get along* can be happier than a single 'too. They serve to keep each other company. I have debated this, but since Benjamin has been alone all of his life, I don't know how he would handle another. I bought him a stuffed U2 as an experiment, and he chewed out the eyes, then pulled stuffing from the head, through the eye holes. It was like a frontal lobotomy. Later, he chewed off a wing. Later still, the belly was opened and the stuffing tossed about the room. Now, granted a living U2 would be able to fight back, but still... It did not give me a warm fuzzy feeling about acquiring a friend for Mr. B. Other U2s I've seen tend to snuggle with their stuffed animals, so... Better safe than sorry, me thinks.

When I make this suggestion, I am doing so with a caveat, voiced in this paragraph. Since you never know if two birds are going to get along, I cannot speak to getting a second bird after you already have the first. Most of the stories I have read, and YouTube videos I have seen, portray situations where a second U2 was brought in, and the two birds did not get along, in some cases fighting intensely. They had to be kept separately, which voids the reason why you acquired a second bird, and only intensifies your responsibilities, cash outflow, and time needed to spend with the birds to keep them emotionally happy and healthy.

I have read that the birds who do get along tend to be siblings. *So the best answer to keeping two U2s is: If the bird you are thinking of acquiring already has a sibling, or a cage or life mate **with whom it gets along**, it would be a great idea to adopt both.* Otherwise, it is a risk.

There is a reason why the bird rescues are turning down U2s everyday due to exceeding capacity. Frustrated, angry 'toos do not make good pets, so they are surrendered to a rescue (or re-homed, or freed to live on their own often in a climate incompatible with their needs).

Many owners do not understand that there are living requirements for these birds that must be abided by, and if they simply made some changes to their situation, they'd probably have a very happy bird. Instead, they think the bird is the problem - it is the one at fault in this "bad relationship" - and they get rid of the bird. Their problem is gone, but the one they created is now in the hands of different people. Someone else has to fix the issues developed by the bird, in order to help the bird be happy - the issues created by people who did not know better.

It's a sad reality that there so many feather-impaired U2s in domestic ownership. Feather plucking is not observed in nature. You don't see a U2 sitting in a tree plucking its feathers or gnawing holes in its skin... I believe a very good reason there are so many angry birds is because they are trapped in a living situation that is far from comfortable, let alone optimal, for them. We, as their owners and potential owners, can change that.

Domesticated animals are those that have been bred for hundreds of years to live in the care of humans. They are distinct from their wild brethren. The majority of birds are not domesticated animals. Even when bred in captivity, most are considered wild. And yet we put them inside our homes, and force them to live by "our rules." Our rules are unnatural for them.

U2s are large birds, meant to fly, meant to live in often massive flocks, habitually spend a lot of time on the ground, and sleep in trees. It's what they are *supposed* to do. It is what their DNA tells them to do. But we tell them to do something different – to live in a manner against their innate needs. Intellectually it confuses them. Based on advice I read in my research, we are supposed to demand that they not to walk on the ground, not chew on things, not snuggle with us... We want them to live the life *we* want them to live, for our pleasure. And that does not, and cannot, work for them. Instead, we need to seek out ways to have what we want, which is their company, while also providing them with what they need for a full life. There are loving Cockatoo owners who go to great lengths to make sure their bird has the right diet so it can live a long life, but then they mistakenly make that long life miserable for the bird because it is rarely allowed to leave its cage. We have to do more...

The Umbrella Cockatoo is such a highly-specialized bird. It is unlike any other. It is even unique among the Cockatoo specie. Bottom line: Oftentimes, people don't truly understand them, think they're like any other bird, and consequently, care provided is not ideal. And the birds suffer. This needs to change.

Our factual information will increase as more and more people are willing to go the extra mile to set up a living situation for their bird that gives them freedom, gives them room to live, and control over their time. And most importantly, one that allows their minds to be active. The Umbrella Cockatoo has not been highly studied in the wild, so as we wait for that to happen, the best thing we can do as U2 owners is share our experience.

Sharing information is not always easy. When it comes to care of any kind, there are always varying opinions - often strong opinions. Putting yourself out there to share your beliefs and practices with others is a precarious position. You are setting yourself up for criticism. However, it truly is the best way for all of us to learn. We simply have to go into our quest for knowledge - both gaining and sharing - with an open mind. What works for one bird, may not work for another. It is no different from any animal of any specie. But by sharing our experience, we can help others grow in their education.

So much of the information out there is from people who have figured things out on their own, as well as from rescues where they have the opportunity to truly watch the birds engage with one another, and live their lives. I don't mean the resuces that keep each bird in an independent cage and sterile environment. No, I'm talking about the wonderful places that put the birds in a very natural environment. I learned some of the most fascinating information from **Cockatoosanctuary.net**, where the founder presents wonderful details on each breed of Cockatoo. She watches them closely, and is doing her best to share with the world all that she has learned from her close observation of their behavior and activities. Everyone should give her pages a read - there is much to be learned from her.

A favorite quote of mine from the Cockatoo Sanctuary site: "We didn't take these beautiful creatures out of their wild flocks, but we live with the aftermath of those who did. Because our pet Cockatoos are just one or two generations out of the wild, they still have wild instincts that affect their behavior. They may not know why they are unhappy but, they know something is wrong. As their guardians, we need to find ways for them to cope."

If we all keep sharing information and learning from one another, eventually, the rescues will no longer be at capacity, because people will be adopting these birds and wisely keeping happy, healthy, satisfied Cockatoos.

BENJAMIN
COMMUNICATION

It has taken me awhile to learn how to communicate well with
Benjamin. But the more time we spend together, the easier it becomes.

Benjamin greets me every time I enter his room. He says either, "Hi Baby"
or "Hey Baby." These are the words I used to greet him each time I went
into his room when we first got him. After a few weeks, he began saying it to
me before I even got the words out. Now, he says it almost every single time
he sees me for a visit. If, on the rare occasion, he doesn't talk, or dance when
I open his door, I know he's possibly in a mood, and might need extra love to
get happy. Either that, or he's simply busy, and I had arrived for a visit at a
bad time.

In the first week we had Benjamin, we were all still getting to know each other. Again, we knew next to nothing, so we were always staring at him the way people stare at monkeys in a zoo. We were constantly trying to figure out what he was trying to tell us in his actions and sounds.

One day in this first week together, while I was hanging out in Benjamin's room, Howy came in. We had a space heater set up to keep the room extra warm since it was April and still quite chilly outside. It had sufficiently warmed the room, so when Howy walked in and was close to the heater, I asked him to please turn it off. He reached down toward the heater and Benji went crazy. He screamed loudly, over and over, scurrying around on his perch, leaning forward, his body vibrating from the intensity of his screams. Shocked by this unexpected drama, Howy stood up quickly before touching the heater, and Benji immediately stopped screaming. He stood still, calm.

Howy sort of chuckled, and reached down to the heater again. Same reaction from Benjamin. Crazy screaming. This time he added wing flapping. Howy turned off the heater and stood back up. Benji went calm again. I wondered aloud if his reaction had anything to do with the heater. Howy bent down to examine it, and Benji screamed again. He continued to scream rapidly and loudly, flapping his wings and sliding back and forth on his perch while Howy looked the heater over. And he saw it – chew marks on the cord, and exposed wiring. Howy quickly unplugged the heater and took it from the room. As soon as he left with the heater, Benji was fine.

In his actions, Benji was trying to let Howy know that the heater was a danger. How cute is that? He was protecting his new dad. What isn't cute is that we had inadvertently, out of sheer naivete, set up a situation where our bird was harmed. My guess is, he could have been killed. He showed no signs of pain or wound, but for him to know that the heater was a danger meant that he was hurt when he chewed on the cord. It had never dawned on either of us that Benji would even notice the cord, let alone chew on it. Day Two of bird ownership was quite a lesson. That was when we had all of the outlets moved up by the ceiling, and kept all cords as far from Benji as possible. Because while he knew that the heater cord was dangerous, it didn't stop him from going after another cord before the electrician arrived. Luckily it was attached to an unplugged floor lamp, so it was just a cord. But it taught me a lesson - not all cords meant danger to Mr. B.

For a good two years, almost every time I told Benjamin no, he would throw a temper tantrum. But at some point, he decided he could be disciplined, and relax afterwards. I'm not sure if perhaps discipline was followed by some kind of punishment in his days before me, but the tone of discipline in my voice seemed to trigger anger in him. And I'm not talking about yelling at him. I merely used a stern tone when I said things like, "No," and "Please don't do that." I'm going to slip a comment into the middle of my story - when it comes to training, using one word for no - generally the word no is best - you can train your bird to understand that it should not be doing what it's doing. Always using the same word is the most efficient manner of training. Since I use various phrases, it isn't the best way, but still works now that we are in tune. He picks up on my tone more often than the words, I think.

And back to the story. After over a year, he seemed to understand that nothing harmful was ever going to follow the discipline, and if he stopped doing what he was doing, I would stop pestering him. And now, while he doesn't always immediately stop what he's doing when I say no, he will stop by the second, or if he's particularly enjoying what he's doing, the third no (or stop it, or please don't...). And there is no temper tantrum, or even a quick mouthing off. Instead, he just goes about new business, or comes over and climbs onto my lap for a snuggle.

I incidentally got one of these reprimands on video. I still watch it to this day because it makes me laugh when he yells at me. I kind of miss it. The mouthing off, I mean – not the tantrums. Those were awful. https://youtu.be/ET0ippARiMA

Benjamin frequently talks to me with his gaze. If he wants something he cannot get to, he simply goes to where that item is, and looks at it. He knows that this will cause me to walk over and get that item for him.
https://youtu.be/NtgrX-LGM1c

He knows that if he dangles from a structure, with his little feet just hanging there in the air as he holds onto the structure with his beak, I will come over and slip my hand underneath his feet.

It is apparent that Benji has studied me almost as much as I have studied him. It's how he knows that I'll come when he dangles, rescue him from a shelf when he doesn't feel like climbing down, pick him up when he lifts his foot, and get things for him that he cannot reach himself. It has also taught him how to manipulate me into staying a bit longer when it's bedtime. Or how to get me to finally give up on something I try to keep him from chewing (assuming that thing isn't really all that important). He is frightening in his ability to remember things, and to manipulate the environment and the people around him. He is smart as a whip...

When he hears the word "bedtime" he immediately tries to get me to play with some toys so I won't leave. Or he will dance and chatter in the cutest fashion, so I'll stick around to watch. If I tell him I have to go feed the horses, he often has a million things he suddenly wants to do before he goes back to his room so I can leave to feed the horses. And when I try to clean, he does his best to distract me - "no, no, come play instead – come kiss me instead – come snuggle with me instead." He is very, very good...

I mentioned that Benjamin chose his name. In his first months, I spent 6-8 hours a day with him in his room everyday. In the first few days, I made a list of names I liked - one for each letter of the alphabet. Then I went through that list reading each name aloud, and watched for a reaction from Benjamin. Whenever I got one, I put a check by that name. The next day I would go over the list of names with checks by them, and would eliminate any that didn't get a reaction. We did this daily until we were down to one. Benjamin. Sure, it's the long way to finding a name, but hey, we had many hours to kill together in his room as we got to know one another. It gave us something to talk about. Plus, I think it's important for any animal in your care to be happy and comfortable around your voice. So I talk to my animals a lot. I read to them, sing to them, and just generally comfort them with my voice, which in turn makes them more comfortable in my presence.

One of our horses dislikes Benjamin with intensity. A horse's sense of hearing is strong, so when I take him outside and he screams, it really sets her off. More often than not, as soon as Zalika sees Benji outside, whether he's screaming or not, she will shoot him a glare of pure disdain. The glare is so powerful you can see it through a fly mask. https://youtu.be/i4PzZ81w95Y

Our other two horses don't mind him much at all. They just go further out in the pasture if he starts screaming. But Zalika is the alpha mare and it is her job to keep her herd safe. She sees Benji as a "problem."

One day I had been reading about vocal cues for horses as I was sitting outside with Benjamin. Howy and I had jumped into horse ownership without any prior knowledge – just like we did with Benji. So I have spent innumerable hours researching Umbrella Cockatoos and horses. As I was reading about how to get a horse to walk, trot, and canter on verbal command, two of the horses walked by in a pasture chute that connects the front yard pasture to one in our back yard. Zalika was in the paddock, and Eli came trotting on down the chute. As I watched Eli, Benji came and sat on my shoulder. A minute later Ayesha was coming up the chute slowly. Suddenly Benji screamed - just a normal U2 scream for no real reason. Ayesha went from a walk to a run, and she ran full tilt all the way to the back pasture, where all of the horses ran together to the stalls while Benji screamed. Benji knows how to make horses move with vocal cues. Go figure. And I actually got it on video! https://youtu.be/YCBWtUxQXx4

Life With Benjamin

Since this is the guy who taught me so much, I would like to share some of the Benjamin stories I have, to sort of display some of the trials, tribulations, and fun in life with an Umbrella Cockatoo. Because I was in the mind space of learning how to care for him, I kept a Benji Journal for awhile. In it, I placed entries of what we did that day, changes in behavior, new things he has done, interesting items of research, entries of what he will eat or won't eat... I did this because I forget things. I'd like to share some entries with you, in the next chapter. I'm not doing this in any kind of celebratory "hey, look at me and my bird" fashion. Any celebrating of U2 ownership should be saved for the folks who have kept a happy U2 for twenty or thirty years and all parties are still smiling.

No, I'm doing it because this time with him is mostly how I learned about him. And what I learned is what I want to share in this book.

Some history: Benjamin was pretty much an impulse buy, completed out of miscommunication. While stuck in bed after a surgery, I saw some YouTube videos of Umbrella and Muloccan Cockatoos. Adorable. I decided I would enjoy adopting one, so I did a bit of research, and shared my interest with my husband. He and I talked about what it would take to add this bird to our already full household of pets, and rather busy life. When I think back to those conversations, and the images I had in my head of what it would be like, I have to laugh. We had it all wrong. I mean seriously - so very wrong.

Anyway, we decided we could fit it in. We prepped our home, got a few cages and perches, some toys, figured out where the bird would stay when I took it with me to the office, and got ourselves ramped up for the new acquisition.

Howy found an Umbrella Cockatoo for sale on Craigslist. We drove almost an hour to visit the bird, and it didn't go well. He climbed up my arm, and I was thrilled. I thought he liked me! He stood on my shoulder for one second, looked at me, and then chomped down on my ear. He did not want to leave his person, and was telling us to go away. He was happy where he was.

Sadly, the wife in this couple who had recently acquired the U2 at a bird show, was having serious lung issues with the dander in the house, so the bird had to be re-homed. You could tell that both the husband and his bird, who were sitting together on the couch when we left, were unhappy with the need for re-homing. It is not an uncommon situation. The woman had many birds, but this was their first Umbrella Cockatoo. They assumed it would be just like all her other birds, but it was not. I wished we could help them out, but I did not feel safe buying the bird after the ear chomp.

As we drove home and I nursed my bleeding ear, I began to re-think this purchase. The bite was a bit of a wake-up call for me. I told my husband I felt I needed to think about this idea more. For some reason, he didn't pick up on the fact that I wanted to wait, and the next day he found another U2 on Craigslist.

He showed me the bird with what I sensed to be some excitement in his voice, and he commented on how cute the bird was. I concluded that he must really want to get one. Always wanting to make my hubby happy, I contacted the seller and asked some questions. She seemed in a hurry to re-home him, and said she would be able to bring the bird to a public location later that same day. Once things were in motion, they just kind of stayed in motion...

 And suddenly, we had Benjamin.

(Ironically, because he missed my intention of wanting to wait on the bird purchase, Howy simply looked for another bird because he thought it would make me happy - not because he wanted one. And I moved forward when I really wanted to wait, because I wanted to make him happy, and thought he really wanted one. You would think twenty years of marriage, and running a business together for nineteen of those years would make us better communicators...)

In Benji's previous home he pulled his feathers out so often that they will never grow back – a common occurrence in U2s. His cage, as you can see in the photo that was in his Craigslist ad, was way too small for him. It's a

fine sleeping cage, but not a sufficient living cage. Due to the plucking, he has very sparse leg feathers, half of the usual number of wing feathers, only down feathers on his chest and back – with coverage sparse at best. And he only has three tail feathers, two on the left side, and one on his right side. He looks as if he's giving a perpetual "rock on" gesture, made famous by the late, great, Ronnie James Dio.

Because he does not have any of the top level feathers that sort of "hold everything together smoothly," he looks very scruffy. But gosh darn it if he doesn't pull it off well. Between the time when he loses his three tail feathers, and the new ones grow out, he looks like a giant white bee. He is way too adorable.

He will never fly, but his wings were still badly clipped when we got him (which could explain his fear of scissors). We had no idea what he truly looked like until we got him home. We picked him up about an hour and a half away from our house, meeting his owners in a restaurant parking lot 45 min from their home. He was in a small cat carrier, and placed in our back seat by his former owner. He was working diligently on chewing his way through the carrier they had put him in. It was no match for his strong beak, and he had several fair-sized holes already started.

He was so frazzled from the car ride he had endured to get to us, that we didn't want to pull him out to take a look at him. We decided it was smarter to just get him home before he ate his way through the plastic carrier. We had no idea what would happen if he were to break out and be free in our car – free, with that dangerously strong beak, in a car with strangers who seemed to be kidnapping him... Besides, what he looked like didn't matter to me. If he had beak and feather disease he would not have lived long, so I might have asked to pay less than what they were asking. But other than that, I just didn't care.

Even with all of my research, I wasn't quite sure how to interact with Benjamin. The videos I had watched were of people who had owned their birds for many years. They and the birds had a relationship of trust. But what do you do before there is trust?

I couldn't really find any information on that question, so I just did what came naturally to me when taking in new animals. We always wind up with rescues - animals that have been in difficult, dangerous, or harmful situations. The quiet approach has always worked well. So I spent many hours with him in his room, just "being there."

We played and talked and hung out. I read to him, and we watched TV together. It was awhile before I tried to touch him, and it was much longer before I let him climb onto me. I had read that you should never let a U2 onto your shoulder, as they will be taller than you which gives them a feeling of superiority, and they can gauge out your eyes. Eeek! So I was paranoid about letting him climb onto my arm, as once on my arm, he wanted to immediately go to my shoulder. Benjamin adores being on shoulders. It is a happy place for him. This caused some initial tension between us. He, wanting to get on my shoulder, while I wanted him to stay away from it. Awkward.

I would say it was easily over a month before I let Benjamin onto my shoulder. And it went well, considering how nervous I was. He was later no longer allowed on my husband's shoulder because each time he was there, Benji would pull off my hubby's glasses. Without his glasses his vision is greatly impaired, so it was not a safe situation. Consequently, the only shoulder Benji has access to is mine, so he's on it often. Again – it's a happy place for him.

Due to the unwanted eyeglass removal service Benji tried to force on him each time my husband spent time with him, Benji's care, maintenance, and entertainment eventually became provided exclusively by me. Benji very quickly went from "our bird" to "my bird." Howy would visit us now and again, but never stay for more than a couple of minutes. Benji would be so wrapped up in wanting to be on Howy's shoulder – he would incessantly hang out at Howy's feet, offering his lifted foot, which is Benji's way of saying, "Please pick me up." Since this request was consistently denied, Benji would get mildly upset, while also continuing to try to change Howy's mind. It got to be annoying for both of them, so Howy stopped hanging out with us for the most part.

Almost exactly a year later, we moved to a new home, where, as I mentioned, we had space set up so Benji could be free, and in the middle of our lives. We were very excited at the thought of having him around – of having him be part of our daily lives and not just settling for time spent with him in his room. Plus it would open up my life if I wasn't spending all of my free time in one room of the house - which frankly was becoming more difficult by the day. I was also very much looking forward to Howy being able to enjoy Benjamin's cuteness and crazy antics. I felt badly that he saw so few of the amazing things Benji did on a daily basis. And we figured if Benji had his play space, he'd not keep trying to get onto Howy's shoulder.

Benjamin was always quiet and well-behaved while in 'Benji's Playhouse' in the basement of our new home, but while in his play space upstairs, he was noisy and obtrusive. We kept trying to make it work for over a year. But it just wasn't. Benji wanted to be in *his* room, not *our* room.

In getting to know him the first year, I spent a good 6-8 hours a day with him in his room, with some of our time spent outside, or in other rooms of the house. That wasn't so much a test of how much time he needed, as a way for me to learn how to read him, and how to care for him. There is nothing like time as a teacher. Plus, in that house, we had 10 cats, so I never felt comfortable being outside of his room with him. If he was with us on a perch in the living room, I was always so closely monitoring the movements of the cats that it was a constant source of stress for me. Many say that a cat won't bother a Cockatoo because they're such a large bird, but I don't know... I saw a couple of cats looking at him as if they were sizing him up as a meal... So we spent most of the time in his room.

At the new house, in his upstairs play space, he'd play on his own just fine for awhile, but never for long. He started getting cranky if I did anything... worked in the kitchen (where he could see me), went to the bathroom, swept or dusted other rooms, sat on the couch (where he could see me) to work on the computer, read a book, or watch tv... I set things up so he could see me when I was outside with the horses. I thought that would make it okay. It did not. He screamed mercilessly the entire time I was outside. When I let him wander, he just chewed on important things, like baseboards, window frames, wall corners. And made impressive messes.

One day he took a bag of grass I'd picked for the horses and threw it all over the floor. It was hilarious, but not fun to clean up.

As I decreased his upstairs time slowly over a few weeks, the time that seemed to work out best was one I never thought would be ideal. When I left him alone in his room to play all day, and went down there between 3 and 5 pm, to stay with him until 7 pm, that seemed perfect for him. He would not

scream at any point in the day. Always in a good mood. Always snuggly.
Always loving. Always playful. My theory is, it's because those hours we
were together were all about Benji, instead of Benji being a part of the things
going on in my life. I might get a task in now and again that had to be done
in the basement, but overall, those Basement Benjiland hours were just me
and Benji, playing and snuggling. It was his favorite thing – attention being
all on him. And he loved his room - it's where all of his stuff was. He could
do whatever he wanted there. That pleased him greatly.

Over time, we changed up our schedule, and now it simply is what it is each
day. It varies. I didn't want to get him into too much of a schedule, just in
case I couldn't always live up to it. I had read that 'toos love a schedule, so I
wanted to see if I could "work around" that attribute. I worried that a lack of
schedule wouldn't work, but lo and behold, it has. I've learned Benji's prime
playing hours, prime napping hours, etc., so I just make sure that I can get
down to him for 2-4 hours throughout the day, working around his naps and
end of day bedtime.

As long as he gets to spend some time with his human, he's a happy boy. The
only thing I have become strict about, is that when he gets sleepy, he is left
alone. This rule is based on the bad ear bite I received when I kept him up
past his bedtime.

As time goes on, I've found that not every single day is perfection. Even
though Benji is, on the norm, a ridiculously happy bird, there are also
occasional days when he's kind of a brat. Nothing pleases him. Only a few
times have they been so bad that I have to leave his room, because being with
him was dangerous. But there are more times when I left because he simply
wouldn't stop screaming. But when I put him in his room and left him alone,
he would be fine. No screaming. I guess all living creatures have moods. I
also found that oftentimes these episodes coincide with the times that he is
sitting on his "egg." He didn't like being away from it.

At first, being a non-flight bird due to his feather loss, I worried about his
falling off of things. And he did. The first was when he was knocked off of
his perch by one of our cats. I did not know then, nor do I know to this day,
if she was jumping up at him, or simply wanted to be on the flat part of the
perch. Either answer fit with her personality. But since the perch was on
wheels, when she jumped up and landed on the perch floor, the whole thing

flew out from underneath her, rolling with an initial jolt. And Benji hit the floor. It was about a 4' drop from the top of the perch. I freaked out. Benji handled it better than I. He was fine.

The next time was when he was temporarily perched on the railing of a spiral staircase. He caught sight of what I thought was a pretty cool pet stroller I had gotten for him. He panicked, screamed, and jumped. He landed on the carpeted floor and ran away. I learned that a running and screaming U2 scares cats more than it intrigues them. Good to know.

When I picked him up, I wondered if it was the stroller that caused that reaction, so I began slowly walking over to it with him on my shoulder. He screamed in panic, and I knew that the pet stroller had to be returned. It was no longer in the cards that I would be the person out for a walk with a bird in a stroller. No idea why Benji had that reaction, but I learned from it. And I marveled at how sharp the frightened "alarm" scream was.

The last fall was more dramatic in fly time. While outside chatting with our neighbors, I had Benjamin perched nearby on a panel of the round pen where we train our horses. A heavy gust of wind came out of nowhere and blew Benji right off the fence. I panicked and ran to him, only to watch him effortlessly and gracefully glide to the ground and land about ten feet from the fence. It was a thing of beauty actually. He was briefly stunned, but then quickly appeared to be quite proud of himself. I learned that he could glide very well, so I didn't have to worry about his falling anymore. Well, truth be told, I will always worry about that, but at least I do so with the knowledge that he can handle himself better than I thought.

Benjamin taught me that attempting to create a fancy place to keep a U2 was more difficult than I had imagined. I have been slowly trying to cover the exterior of 'Benji's Playhouse' with soft textured fake brick panels. I thought it would look fantastic, so that the exterior of his house wasn't just a bunch of drywall panels. Because it's working on his house, it's not something that can be done while he's inside the playhouse. He will not stand for someone being outside of his house without including him in whatever activity is going on at the time. So it had to be done with Benji running around in the play space. This is why I decided to use easy-to-install adhesive panels rather than something more complicated.

Two flaws in that plan. While they are adhesive, so should go on quickly and easily, working on putting them up meant that I was not watching or playing with Mr. B. Consequently, he would try to distract me in any way that he could. Getting one panel on with any precision at all was difficult, let alone eighty of them. Even if I successfully got one up, it had to be moved a few times to get it in the right place, since I often had a bird sitting on my leg or shoulder at the time, trying to bite the panel – and they'd eventually lose their adhesion from being pulled off over and over. I ordered the panels in November of 2018. It is now July of 2020, and I'm not even half done. To make matters worse, many of the panels that I did get up were not pressed on hard enough due to Benjamin climbing the ladder to be with me, or distracting me. So I'm usually pressing them down daily. And secondly, those that are well-adhered now have beak shaped holes in them. Yes, he loves to chew on the panels. So... there's that.

Inside, I hung a beautiful cloth mural on the wall behind his perch. It was a very realistic photograph of a beautiful wooded scene. It covered one of the short walls of his room in its entirety and looked utterly fantastic. https://youtu.be/DxBk6yzMTg8

It took him less than fifteen minutes to chew a massive hole in it, and another ten to rip sections off of the wall. https://youtu.be/0GUTOVRUlZ

I wanted his house to look amazing. Like a little modern cottage in our basement. Instead, it looks like the house of an Umbrella Cockatoo – tattered and chewed. I finally let my ideal plan go, and stopped reprimanding him for chewing on the exterior. I figure, it is his house, and if that's what he wants, who am I to demand anything else?

They say that U2s need twelve straight hours of sleep each night. Without the structure of another's schedule influencing his, and without a blanket tossed over a cage as is done with most birds, Benji does what his body and mind want to do. And for awhile, both seemed to want to be up and active for many hours of every day and night. I'm not sure why, but for awhile, he was all about the play, and not so much about the sleep. It eventually passed, and he went back to a pretty normal schedule. But every now and again, I can hear him playing at midnight. The late night playtimes are generally in winter months when the sun goes down before 5:00pm. He sleeps when the sun goes down, and wakes up in the middle of the night. He plays for awhile, and then sleeps again until around 8:00 or 9:00am. I guess it's not that different from our "midnight snacking sessions."

In my research, I read that some birds are actually afraid of the dark. The sheet over their cage is supposed to block out all light, and make them feel safe. For some birds, it makes them tense, even nervous. If you choose to go the sheet over the enclosure route, it's probably a good idea to check on your bird now and again when you first begin doing this, to make sure it isn't frightened..

Lastly, a quick look at Benji's more controlling side: Oftentimes, when Benji and I spend our time together, he sets the tone. He decides what we're going to do, and if I try to deviate from his plans, I am set straight... If I take him outside on my shoulder and he doesn't want to be there, he either screams, bonks my cheek with his beak, or simply climbs off of me and walks back to the house where he waits at the door for me to let him back inside. Rarely can I entice him to play outside if he doesn't want to be there. While inside, if he's busy playing a solo game and I walk away to do something else (play with a toy, clean his room, sweep the play space, rearrange things...), he will run to me and request that I come back to watch him some more. Or, he will bring me a toy so he and I can play together. Or, he will simply scream. And if I'm playing with one of his toys, there is a good chance that he will take it away from me. He doesn't like it much when my attention is placed elsewhere, even if he was just happily playing on his own. Benji time must be exactly that – Benji time. And Benji's toys are exactly that - *Benji's* toys.

In the set up that we have, and the way that we have arranged our lives together, while this behavior can sometimes be annoying, it's also okay. I give Benji 2-4 hours each day, and he is left alone the other 20-22 hours. When viewed that way, I can completely understand his need to have all of my attention for the entire time I am with him. And so I give it to him. He will eventually allow me enough time to get done the important cleaning tasks that I need to do in his area, even if it means that I do my part in a game, sweep a bit, and then play my part again. Back and forth. Benji – clean – Benji – clean. It all works out.

But this behavior may not work in another setting – say if the bird is living in the midst of the family. This is one of the reasons I really love the arrangement we have. The fact that Benji is alone, and yet happy for the majority of each day is astounding. He loves his room, and he plays in it quietly, willingly, and joyously. When I'm there for him – awesome! Fun and snuggles abound! When I'm not there – that's okay. He's still happy. While not everyday is perfect, the vast majority are. It is proof to me that yes, U2s need significant time with their people, but it's manageable in the right circumstances. And I believe that letting him be who he is, in a safe and loving environment, is just the answer.

THE JOURNAL

I would like to share some information from my journal entries, to show you what I experienced in my life with Benjamin. These are from April 2019 to September 2019. In September I began writing a book about horses, so my daily Benji and horse journals were unfortunately pushed to the side.

This chapter goes on for some time. It's pretty much half of the book. If you're interested in stories of the "day to day" then please, read on! But if it's not of interest, I suggest you hop on to the last chapter, which shares extremely useful thoughts from others who are owned by U2s.

And on to the journal entries...

◆ ◆ ◆

I had a banana nut muffin – nibbling on it now and again while we played outside of his room. He noticed it. He stopped playing, and waddled over to me. He gave me "The Look." I held the muffin in front of him. He nibbled on it. Liked it. I broke a small piece off for him – he ate it and requested more. I broke off another small piece and offered it to him. He instead reached past it, took my big piece, and left me with the small bit. He walked away to eat it a good 7 feet from me so I'd not try to take it back.

◆ ◆ ◆

I pulled out the five milk crates I got at St. Vincent's today, and set them up in two stacks - one of 2 and one of 3. Benji climbed up the stack of two, and it held him very well, although I was holding on to it to be sure. It didn't teeter at all. I made a mental note to go back tomorrow morning to get more. He really enjoys them, and it would be a nice way to store some of his toys.

When he was done hanging out on this tiny tower, we wandered around, with him on my shoulder, just looking at stuff again, deciding where to put things as we reorganized his space for the sake of variety, as well as deciding where to put the crates. When I set him down, I took one of the milk crates over to the section of the basement where I have boxes, bags, baskets and totes all holding his inventory of "back-up" toys. I started moving some of the toys to the milk crates.

Did he ever have fun with that! Seeing all those toys... It was almost more than he could bear. He climbed around on the milk crates, pulling toys out and throwing them around, playing with them, looking at them and then tossing them back into the crate. I found a part of a deck of a cards in one box, so I put those into a crate. He pulled them out of the crate and threw them around. I picked them up, spread them out in my hand and told him to "pick a card, any card." He picked 3, and walked away with them. I tossed some cards around and he chased them, then picked up a few and chewed on them. I rolled a matchbox car to him and he rolled it back to me. I rolled it again, he picked it up, turned it over as he examined it, and then dropped it. Game over.

I would hand him toys and he would either play with them, drop them, or refuse them by turning his little head in the opposite direction. He climbed up the milk crates, which gave him the height to get inside a large box of styrofoam balls. He climbed into the box, and began throwing balls out. The first two he threw ricocheted off the side flap of the box and went directly into the waste basket. Amazing. He followed those with tosses that went every which way. Then he climbed out and played with other toys for awhile. I put the balls he'd tossed, back into the box. I then added to the box some thick display board I had picked up today and had cut up into smaller chunks. He climbed back into the box and threw those, and more balls out again. He loves throwing things.

Howy came down and Benji got so excited. He talked rapidly and used his wings for emphasis often. Howy used a small metal pole to tap out some beats on one of the support beams, and Benji danced to it – bopping and flinging his head around. A hoot. Howy and I stepped outside to discuss a yard project, and B followed us out. He brought with him a thick metal (hollow) pole that he enjoys throwing around. He threw it at us, I threw it back, he threw it again, I threw it again, and then he walked to me with it in his beak, and asked to get on my shoulder. I brought him up, and he accidentally bonked me in the face with it on his way up – not a surprise. He held on to it and then asked to get onto my hand - something he does by simply leaning forward. I lifted my hand, he got on and readjusted the pole, and then climbed back on my shoulder. Once situated, he took it from his beak and just stood there holding it in his foot. Eventually he dropped it, then sat on my shoulder looking around at the horses, and the cars going by.

I started to tell Howy about the balls Benji threw, which went into the wastebasket, and B kept interrupting me. I said, "Okay, why don't you tell him what happened." I hadn't gotten to the exciting part, so I waited for him to tell it. He just looked at me. I said, "Alright, I'll tell him," and I started to do so. B interrupted me again. Howy and I laughed, and B laughed. "Hahahahaha."

When we went back inside, Howy stuck around for a bit, and B snuggled up to his leg, feathers up, shivering with happiness. He so adores Howy. Howy bent over and petted him, and B just looked sooooo happy.

I showed Howy how Benji could move the 10 lb weight. Benji rolled it around, and then over to me. I handed it to Howy, and he felt how heavy it was. He marveled at the tiny Hulk that is Benji. I was going to show him how B would run at, and knock over the big weight, but instead, B just walked to it and tapped it. He was mellowing, which was good since it was almost bedtime.

B ran to his room to get his peanut butter sandwich. He came out holding it in his beak, which made Howy laugh. I told B to keep eating his sandwich, and I was going to take Howy to the back to show him what we had worked on earlier. Howy and I were back there for less than a minute when B came back, toting half a sandwich in his beak. He stopped a few feet away from us, and ate there. Just wanted to be close. He then walked over to me, put out his foot, and I picked him up. He finished the sandwich on my shoulder. Howy left, and B wiped his beak in my hair. Gross. Yet weirdly endearing.

Sometimes a day calls for two showers when you have a 'too.

After Howy left, we went to B's room and got situated for bedtime. B talked a lot, used his intense wing emphasis, and ran back and forth from under his cage, to me, then under his cage, and then to me... He would run out each time I had finished a task and it looked as if I might leave. I sat down with him for a few minutes, and we chatted. I think he was telling me what a marvelous time he had today, and I told him I did too.

He finally went into his man cave and stayed there when I stood up. He peeked out as I was walking toward the door, and he ran out and grabbed his grape. He ran to the door with it as I was slowly closing the door, telling him goodnight and to enjoy his grape. Watching him through the window in the door, I saw he ate the grape. He kept talking to me as I turned on his music, turned off the lights, and headed to the basement door. He screamed his nightly shout out to his flock a couple of minutes later.

He danced and sang and screamed at horses and played with a million toys today. It was a very good day.

Another fine day with Mr B. Howy and I had picked up another 11 milk crates. Howy took them down to Benji's play space when I went downstairs for a visit. I let Benji out, and he was very excited to see Howy down there with us. He sat on my shoulder and bounced around with his crest up, showing off for Howy as he always does. Howy didn't stay long though – just dropped the crates off, and took up a box of DVDs to go through before they went to the charity garage sale.

B and I played with the big weight for awhile – the 10 lb one. Just rolled it around a bit, and I held it up on its side a few times so he could run at it and knock it down. I had to do some cleaning. The messes we made yesterday in our organizing tasks were still around, so I did some sweeping and putting things in their places. I grabbed one of the milk crates, and started putting some of his styrofoam balls into it. He enjoyed that! He climbed up on the side of the milk crate, and as I put balls into it, he grabbed them and threw them out. Ball in, ball out. Ball in, ball out. Like shoveling sand. I took the box of styro balls and held it on its side, tipping the box so the balls would roll toward the milk crate. B climbed from the side of the crate to the top and reached over into the box with his neck extended. He began pulling balls from the box, pushing and tossing them into the crate, and all around the room.

He climbed into the box as I held it, and he started kicking the remaining balls with his feet, backwards into, and around, the crate. He kept this up for awhile, climbing around inside the large box, around the rim of the crate, etc.

I rearranged some items to make room for a short milk crate "wall." I built the wall with most of the 11 crates, and he immediately started to climb it. I put the crates containing styro balls on the top. He climbed up to the top and began throwing balls around again. I got some video of this, and the other stuff above – but the activities listed above comprise a long video, and it appears I didn't have the phone set up high enough to get the fun box stuff. You can only see his bottom half. It was my first attempt at "still video" and I didn't know what we'd be doing. That's a problem with still video - you never know where the action is going to happen, until it does. I assumed all fun things done by Benji would be on the ground. I had great ground coverage with the camera. But instead, most of the fun stuff was done at a higher level. It's basically video of his hind end having a good time.

When he was done on the crate, he climbed down, and I began some sweeping. I've debated throwing out a small container of dirt, but he had so much fun with it when I first brought it in, that I've been keeping it just in case he wants to play with it again. He hasn't touched it in months. Today was the day I decided to throw it out. I reached for it, and he ran over. He immediately began rummaging through the dirt with his beak and feet. I got video of him throwing the dirt all over. I guess the pail of dirt will last awhile longer. At least until the next time I debate throwing it out.

I put Benji back in his room while I went to feed the horses. B was tired, and slowing down, so it was a good time to take a break.

B was screaming a little bit when I got back inside. I waited for a quiet moment, then headed down and opened his door. He said "hi baby" happily, and climbed from his perch onto my shoulder. I stayed with him until almost 7. We played with many things, and cleaned up messes we made earlier in the day. At one point he went to the windows of the exterior doors and looked out. I tossed a toy to him, and he ignored it. He looked at me, and then back out the window. He wanted to go outside. I told him it was super windy out, but if he wanted to try it, that was fine.

I opened the door, and he walked out. Once out there, he walked ahead of me, stopped and looked around, and then put his foot out. I find it so amusing how sometimes he doesn't even look at me when he does that. He's like a king, offering his hand for the kiss of a loyal subject - eye contact would not be suitable.

So here he is, scoping out the landscape, lifting his foot and expecting his own personal Uber-shoulder transport to appear beside him and pick him up. And of course, it did. I slid my hand under his foot and swooped him onto my shoulder. We walked to the pine trees. I thought that the wind break of the trees would be good, plus there was some sunshine there. I invited him to climb down my arm to the ground, but he didn't take me up on it. So I sat down, and he sat on my shoulder for awhile longer.

When he finally got down, he went under a pine tree, dug a small hole, but didn't stay long. He came back to me and snuggled on my lap. Then it was back up on my shoulder. I got up after awhile and walked to the round pen to see if he wanted to get on the gate. I thought maybe the wind would be a bit lighter, since perhaps the house would also offer a break. It wasn't too bad.

He climbed on, walked around, sang a bit, and I took his picture.

I sliced open some hay bales that were to go into the compost pile. B came down off the gate and climbed up a bale to see what I was doing.

He climbed onto my arm. I lifted him up and suggested he nibble on some tall weeds. And he did, for quite awhile. When he was done, he went back to my shoulder and sat there, soaking up sun, for quite some time. He climbed down to my arm and nibbled on weeds again - short weeds this time. Then he got down, and walked around on the ground. I pulled some weeds and laid the velvet leaf stalks nearby so I could pull the leaves off for Eli – he loves the velvet leaf leaves. The girls don't like them, and spit them out when offered to them. But Eli will slide his long horsie head through the fence to get to them. I'm glad he does, as they're very nutritious.

While I was pulling leaves off, B came over and got on my shoulder again. We pulled leaves together for awhile, but as soon as I told him I was doing that for Eli, he lost interest. I don't think he cares for the horses much. He got down, and walked over to the gate, where he climbed up, shuffled across, and then climbed down onto the wooden bench. He took a chunk out of the bench with his beak – his way of indicating he wasn't getting enough attention.

I finished pulling the leaves off of the plant I was working on, grabbed the pile and took it to the door. I went back, grabbed the plants I'd picked for Benji to tear apart inside, and then got him. We went back inside.

We played with various items, but he was starting to show some crankiness. He was tired.

He rolled the 10 lb weight to me. This was the 4th time he'd rolled it. I'm getting video of this: He rolls it to me, I roll it back, he runs under his cage, pops back out, rolls it to me, runs back to his room and chews on the door flap. I ask him not to do that. The door flap is what keeps the heat inside his room. He doesn't stop. I get closer to him, wiggle a small piece of paper near him to get his attention, and I tell him to stop doing that. He stops, and steps away. I thank him. He says something to me. I say, "I know you know no." And he yells at me! It sounds like perhaps whatever he said to me a second ago was what he said again, only louder and with some force. It's hilarious. Then he goes into his room and starts screaming. He keeps screaming. I laugh, I try to distract him, and while I do, it only lasts for a few seconds, and then he's screaming again. I put him to bed. What a hoot he is. https://youtu.be/ET0ippARiMA

◆ ◆ ◆

I went back down at 215, and planned to stay until 5 or a bit later. However, I left at 440. He went into a screaming jag, so I walked into his room, he followed, I told him I loved him and I'd see him in the morning. I left and shut the door. He stopped screaming. I hate it when our nights end like that, but with me there he would not stop screaming. That scream grates on nerves like sliding on your knees on concrete. It's unnerving and weirdly painful. We had a lot of fun up to that point though. It was too windy to go outside but we did sit in the open doorway for maybe 5 minutes to get a little fresh air. We mostly played with the round weight. I got some video. He also looked at himself in the mirror for a long time. I thought I got it on video, but when I looked down after a minute or so, it wasn't recording. I have to silence the phone so he won't know when I turn it on. Otherwise, he stops doing anything at all once he hears the click of the camera turning on. Sadly it also means that I don't know when I think I've turned it on but actually haven't.

Luckily he did it again so I did get a bit of B checking himself out. A bit later he sort of peeked back to the mirror. I couldn't tell if he knew he was looking at himself, or if he thought there was another bird in the room. Either way he didn't react much. That in and of itself was interesting. He's also been chewing on the frame of the mirror, and it appears he somehow scratched the mirror face itself. It's one of those children's mirrors, princess-themed, all plastic and just shiney foil-like material for the mirror. I can only imagine the trouble he could get into if I gave him a real mirror. It pains me to think what biting on a real mirror could do to him. This mirror, we learned, speaks to you if you press a button - a button we didn't know was there. Benji pressed it while chewing on the frame, a voice came out of it, and both Benji and I jumped. It startled us!

When we went back to playing, he rolled the weight to me – it didn't come close enough so I asked him to roll it a bit closer. He did, and then turned and began walking away. He turned around ever so slightly sort of mid-step, and said, "K?" Like, "Is that good? Close enough?" I said, "It's great – thank you." He finished his walk to the box and waited for me to roll it in there. It was just so human.

I went into his room to get things set up for my having to leave and feed the horses. B was running around in the room with the weight. He brought it to me, and I rolled it. He ran after it and brought it back. I was laying down newspaper. I laid the paper, then without looking, reached over to pick up the weight – sadly at the same time that B reached for it. My finger was bitten HARD. Deep and bleeding profusely. Fun! Just ten days ago he had bitten me – again accidentally during the rolling of the weight. Same darn spot. It just finished healing the day before yesterday. And now I'm back to limited use of my dominant hand. So annoying. Hopefully it won't swell up as badly as that last bite did. I couldn't bend my finger for days.

Analyzing why it happened – I wasn't paying attention, it was toward the end of our visit so he was tired, and when he gets tired he gets clumsy and aggressive and hyper-active. That's when I really have to pay attention. So really a trifecta situation – inattention, tired, hyper-active. Gotta keep a better eye on things...

Howy fixed up Benji's new weight. B had chewed off bits of the plastic coating, which left tiny sharp edges here and there. Those could cut into his cheek when he would roll it around on the ground. So Howy covered it neatly in gorilla tape. Benji immediately pulled some of it off, but it should last a few days before we have to coat it in tape again – the Gorilla tape in multiple layers really holds up well to the U2 beak. I can't leave the barbell in his room though, as he would have the tape off long before morning. We will exclusively play with it in the play area, so I can keep an eye on it. I'd rather he didn't play with it in his room even if I'm there, because I have a hard enough time remembering the 10 things I have to check before I leave him for the night. I don't want to make it 11, and then forget.

◆ ◆ ◆

He played a lot with various toys, keeping himself busy all afternoon. I actually got a few things done. I also got some good video: https://www.youtube.com/watch?v=HJqHk8IYbdw

◆ ◆ ◆

When I was trying to fix one of Benji's feathers that is somehow turned so it sticks out on his chest instead of shaped to the curve of his chest... I said, "what is up with this feather?" Benji responded with something I couldn't decipher, but it had the word feather in it.

When I went back down at 530, I had more fun with Benji than I think I ever have in our time together. It was pee-your-pants fun. He was HILARIOUS.

While in his room he was in almost constant Cockatoo chatter with expressive wing gestures. At one point, I was brushing a fly away. Unbeknownst to me, B came up from behind me and I wound up bumping him in the chest with my hand as I swiped at the fly. He walked away, saying, "I just got hurt." I swear it. And while I feel badly about it, and immediately apologized to him, I could not help but laugh myself to tears. And then I kept hearing it over and over in my head, his tiny voice saying, "I just got hurt." So even after I stopped laughing initially, I'd wind up laughing again. His voice is sooo adorable. Benji was under his cage, looking out and laughing back at me.

Later, he was standing on my leg, and pushing the weight over each time I'd stand it on end. He'd push it, I'd set it back upright, he'd push it down, I'd set it back up, over and over again. Then he reached for the plastic stick, so I handed it to him. He played with it while continuing to sit on my leg, moving the stick around with his foot, turning it this way and that, putting it in his beak... then he tossed it, as he does. He's sitting there, on my leg, and he reaches his foot out toward the stick, wiggles his toes, and says, "Hand that back to me." I'm not kidding! I feel like I'm losing my mind. I really do. I have to get this stuff on video so Howy can see that they're really happening, but you just never know when they'll happen. And when I have the camera in front of me filming him, it either inhibits him greatly, or he just tries to eat it.

"Hand that back to me." Ha! I still laugh about it!

It's impossible to stay in a bad mood when you're cheering on a bird. I spend most of my time with B saying things like, "Woohoo!" and "Look at you go!" and "What a good/smart/strong boy!" And when we play games I make a lot of sound effects that I wouldn't even know how to spell. B and I had a very good time, and he talked a lot – especially when we went into his room again. Went in at 415 to check his papers, sweep up a bit, and make sure things were in order. He followed me in, brought in his weight, and wanted to play there. I don't know why, but he really likes being in there. I figured he'd want to get out of there whenever possible since he's in that room all night. But no, he just loves it there.

He decided he didn't want me cleaning at all. Normally he just tries to distract me when I clean up his hoarding messes. But today as I picked up the papers, and laid new ones down around the cage to catch his poos, he jumped in front of me, talked and talked, and then climbed up the cage to dangle off the corner at head height so he could look at me, eye to eye. I broke out laughing, and kissed the top of his head.

I've been too wiped to write in this journal everyday, but I do want to write about a couple of things that have happened the last few days.

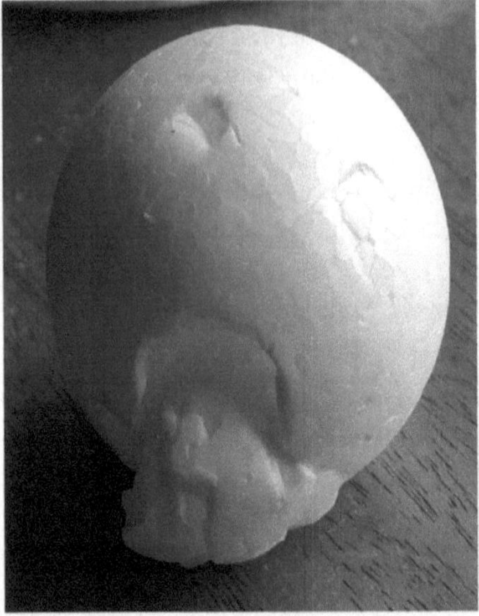

I found a styrofoam ball that had rolled behind a shelving unit. Benji had bitten it, and it looks hilariously like a vomiting emoticon, or emoji - I honestly don't know the difference, but this looks like one of them. It seems I have an artist in my midst...

At one point B held on to the side of the 3-level wire rack with his beak, and dangled his feet, wiggling them around. But it wasn't in the "mom come and get me" manner he usually does. He stays still for that. This was more like a dance. Sort of a swish swish kick, swish swish kick. You could have set it to music.

I had a bag of mini marshmallows from which I was eating while sitting on the ground playing with him. He came over and got up onto my knee. He took the bag from me, held it in his claw and beak, and turned it several times until it was upside down. He shook it so all the marshmallows fell out. Then he jumped off my knee and landed in the middle of the mallows. He threw them, one by one, around him, wiggling his wings in excitement with each throw. I picked them all up and put them back in the bag when he was done. He came over and reached into the bag with his beak to pull them out, one by one again, and tossed them in a circle around him.

I laid the new climbing gate down on its side so it was flat on the ground. I wanted to see if the rug I got was going to cover the whole thing (it won't). I was seeking some way to allow him to climb up one side, but not climb down on the other side – in order to create a barricade so he can't get to the car-storage side of the basement. I thought the rug would work. When I laid the rug on the gate, he walked and ran up and down it like it was a red carpet. He brought some of his toys up onto it to play with them there. Something new – something exciting.

He's been strangely neat lately, barely messing up his room. Weird.

◆ ◆ ◆

Lots of snuggles later in the afternoon. Still played a lot, mostly outside of his room this time. When the song "Rock Lobster" by the B-52s came on, B was on my lap getting snuggles. As soon as the song started – and this is the first time he's ever heard it – he sat upright, spread his wings a little bit, bounced dramatically on my leg, and then jumped off and ran around in his kinda-dance mode. It was highly amusing. He played hard during the song. Music can really affect his behavior. Later that afternoon he came over and sat on my leg, looked at me, and spread his wings as wide as they could go and made the funniest sound. Like a loud HNNNNNN. Then he flapped his wings a wee bit, jumped off my leg, and went back to play. He was showing off. I got a kick out of it.

◆ ◆ ◆

Good Benji day. Was down with him for 2-2.5 hours and it seemed much shorter. He let me get a few things done in between playing. I was able to sweep, and then roll the weight when he'd bring it by. He followed me around a lot, talked to me while I cleaned, leaned in for kisses (trying to distract me...). He danced while I clacked and rubbed the rhythm sticks together. No outside time – too windy. He talked a lot today.

I went behind his playhouse to do some sweeping. The space is blocked with a thick plastic children's playhouse set up – gate, mailbox, etc. He tried to get back there with me and was getting frustrated when he couldn't. Since I had all the electrical cords up high, I figured it was safe, so I opened the gate and he joined me. He immediately began chewing on the insulation. Regret. We finished back there and went back to games in the play space. Later, he walked over to the little gate, opened it with his beak, and headed behind his playhouse on his own. He remembered how I'd opened it, grabbed the top with his beak and just pulled it open. Too smart. And now that can no longer be considered a barrier to keep him from that area. Must find new barrier.

He made a request for the peanut butter jar, and of course, I complied: https://www.youtube.com/watch?v=NtgrX-LGM1c

◆ ◆ ◆

He danced, ran around, did some head banging, hopped a lot, threw the new toy around, and got himself pretty worked up. We went into his room to get ready for bed. As soon as he knows it's time for me to leave he tries to convince me to stay. Breaks my heart. I'd be more open to staying later if I didn't fear a bad bite as he gets tired.

He doesn't seem to know, or want to admit when he's tired. Then he gets clumsy and more worked up, and eventually bites me. They're generally accidents, and we're both to blame. But once bitten I'm either in the ER or in pain for days. And other than that bad ear bite he gave me right before Halloween, which definitely was not an accident, it's always my right hand index finger that gets bitten – same finger, same placement on the finger, same reason for the bite. Since the last one is at least the fifth in that exact same spot, the scar tissues are sort of bundling up and creating a lump – a painful lump. The knuckle is all convoluted, and I can't straighten the finger as well as I can the left. Good times, good times.

◆ ◆ ◆

He came out of the room, and we played on the new mat I got at St Vincent's yesterday. Well worth the $4! On one side there are squares with animals in them which correspond to the letters of the alphabet. On the other side, it's an oceanscape with cartoon fish, teddy bears on jet skis, stuff like that. Benjamin has a thing about gauging out the eyes of his stuffed animals... This act is apparently not limited to stuffed items. He was walking around on the mat looking at the pictures, and he bent down and began chewing on the eyes of the cartoon fish. I had to laugh. What is it with him and eyes??

Which reminds me, the other day while on my shoulder, he leaned in slowly, heading carefully toward my eye, and he tried to touch it with his tongue. I laughed, closed my eye, and said, "I don't think so..."

When we roll the weight around, I spend a lot of time saying, "Good one" when he rolls it to me. This afternoon, he said, "Good one" when I rolled the weight to him.

I found the spot in which I wanted to put the couch we were bringing down to Benji's play space. I'd also like to eventually move the bird cage from upstairs down there, just to get it out of the dining room. But first, all of the empty moving boxes in this basement space have to be removed. So I grabbed a bunch, and began tearing them down. Thought I could do that, roll the weight, break down a box, roll the weight, and hopefully at some point B would go off on his own for some independent play, so I could clear that area and prep for the couch. Turns out I could not. B wanted the knife. B wanted each box. B didn't want me to move the boxes. B wanted me to just play, and leave everything as it was. He ran around, chased me, yelled at me, tried to distract me, screamed, climbed inside boxes and refused to come out... the usual process of Amy trying to get something done down there. I got about 5 boxes broken down and then decided to just chuck a bunch into the stairwell, take them upstairs, and break them down in the garage.

While B and I were on the floor rolling the weight, Howy showed up and knocked on the exterior door. He was there with the couch! I wasn't ready! I cleared a space for it near the glass doors. There are two glass doors and a door-sized pane of glass there. When you open the two doors and removed the pane of glass you can drive a car through - the basement was set up for car storage. We opened one door and took out the pane of glass so the couch would fit through. Benji screamed like crazy the entire time. He so hates chaos that is not caused by him.

I tried to calm him but it was no use. So I cleaned up, tossed more boxes into the stairwell, made sure his room was set up, and put him inside, where he made all sorts of blender noises. The blender noises are ones he makes when he's just hanging out by himself. They're actually weirdly similar to the noise made by Kaykao, the antagonist in the movie, "The Grudge." And, sometimes they sound like our blender, which he used to hear every morning at the other house when I made my smoothies.

Howy and I saw a commercial with an Umbrella Cockatoo on it, and I commented on how different Benjamin looks than a Cockatoo who has a tail. Howy called B "the Flightless Penguin Cockatoo" or the Cockaguin. I suggested the Penkatoo. Howy liked that one better.

B did his evening "going to bed" set of screams at exactly 8:00. Done screaming at 8:03.

◆ ◆ ◆

We went outside right away, and he sat on the round pen, wandered around, walked with his beak down on the railing rubbing it along the way, sang, screamed, and posed for some wonderful photos. We played with his weight for awhile, snuggled a wee bit, he dug a couple of holes in the ground with his beak, and then we walked to the pine trees. He went under several trees and picked up pine needles to throw around. Eventually he walked to the compost pile and dug around in there for awhile.

He threw some pine shavings around, threw some horse poo, chewed on a few pieces... Thank goodness they're old poos and are mostly just rounded cubes of grass now. We were outside for almost 2 hours. I put him back in his room at 5 and headed out to feed the horses.

He is so smart. If you ask him to go get his weight, he will go get it! He repeats doing anything that will make you laugh. He danced, snuggled, played with a bunch of toys, hung out on his gate... He had a really good time. As did I! I put him to bed at 7:00. I toss his weight in, he goes in after it, and I close the door – and every time he looks at me with the saddest, somewhat surprised expression on his face. I prefer the nights when he and I are in his room together for awhile before I leave. It gives him time to hunker down in his man cave so he doesn't care as much that I leave. This day went on too long for that I'm afraid.

He was very noisy today. Screaming outside, screaming inside, multiple times. It's unusual. Some singing, some laughing, but mostly screams. Not angry screams. Just U2 screams. I watched him a bit in the baby monitor after leaving him for the night. He went to his perch 2x - both times before 8. Never seen that before...

♦ ♦ ♦

We did a lot of work around the yard, painting and moving compost, so I didn't get in to see Benji until 3. We immediately went outside, and had a wonderful time. It was super windy, so his feathers blew all over and made cool sounds. Now and again he would hide under my arm or in my lap. For awhile he snuggled up into my arms and I held him until the wind died a bit. A portion of the round pen was taken down, so it was only half the usual number of panels. He wandered the half that was still up, but spent most of his time on the ground. Wandered far away from me 2x. He's getting braver all the time. We picked weeds out of the flower bed on the side of the house. He helped me by walking into the flower patch and picking some weeds with his beak. When he climbed onto my shoulder I had to hand him each weed when I picked it so he could chew it in half. It takes longer, but he has fun. When I can get things done AND he can have fun, well that's just the best thing ever.

Maybe an hour and a half later he wanted to go inside, where we played for awhile. I put him back in his room so I could go feed the horses. I went back at 520 and stayed with him until he went on a screaming spree, which was at around 550. I picked up his weight and tossed it into his room. He is so totally on to that ploy. He ran over to the door, and then stopped, dead in his tracks, standing right outside the door next to me, refusing to go in. He looked up at me and said "Pretty bird" a few times, in his cute little voice. I gave him some kisses and told him he was the best bird. I tried giving him a nudge but he wouldn't go in. I tossed a roll of tape in, and he followed it, then turned and glared at me when I closed the door. I doubt he'll fall for that again.

♦ ♦ ♦

I had Howy come down to help me get the couch off the dolly once I had it moved to the new "sitting area." Benji was so happy to see him. He was screaming out of annoyance that I was rearranging his play space when I called Howy down. Howy walks in and Benji starts singing instead, and spreading his wings in happiness. It's hard being the caretaker sometimes...

While we were in his room and I was cleaning a few things, he kept trying to distract me again and it made me laugh so hard. He runs in front of me, or steps on the thing I'm trying to clean up, or leans in for a kiss or just talks incessantly while standing in front of me and I just laugh and laugh. Heso gosh darn cute.

◆ ◆ ◆

Benji was sweet as could be. Very snuggly, sometimes playful, and always wonderful. I've decided to write a "Caring for Benji" manual, in case anything happens to me and he needs to go to a new home. It is one of my nightmares. I know Howy thinks I'm insane for even thinking about it, but I'm a planner by nature...

◆ ◆ ◆

We played and snuggled as usual – delightful. There was a small amount of time when he was rolling the bigger weight to and from his big box, when he got kind of hyper. Like weirdly so – almost edgy and mean, but not quite. When we stopped playing with that, he calmed down immediately. Interesting...

The cutest thing... At one point he was sitting on my leg while I was on the floor. He reached over and took my right hand forefinger into his claw, and wrapped his fingers around it. He was "holding my hand." He then leaned in and laid his head on my chest. He laid there like that for a few minutes while I petted him with my left hand. Then I had to cough and he took off. Normally, if I keep my hand on his back when I cough, he will stay. But sometimes he will hop away, as if the cuddle spell has been broken. Ironically I'm usually coughing because of his powder, but he doesn't need to know that.

◆ ◆ ◆

Benji loves the sound of drumming. I drum and he dances. He also loves it when I lightly tap the drumstick on his beak a few times, as part of my drumming. When I drum, I usually drum on various things to get different sounds, so I'll tap a few times on the floor, then his beak, then on the rug, then his beak, then on the fence... So I'm sitting still but moving all around to reach these different items. Normally he just stands on my leg, and I'll tap out som beats. Today, he's sitting on my leg and I'm drumming, adding his beak into the beat. I tapped his beak 2x and then instead of staying there and waiting for me to get back to him after drumming elsewhere – he moved elsewhere! He moved 2 steps up my leg and extended his neck the way he does before I tap his beak. I tapped it again, and he moved up 2 steps and invited me to tap his beak again... He was moving to different areas the same way I do when I drum! Bug in a rug he is. Bug... in... a... rug.

◆ ◆ ◆

Went down in the morning. Howy outside doing project using tractor so b screamed a lot - he doesn't like loud engines. Tried to distract. Nothing worked. Exceptionally loud and single-mindedly tenacious. Finally left to get away from lthe noise. Back later. Still screamy but not as bad. Left again. Better when I returned. We sang together. He stole the best dorito out of my bowl n took it to his box. Dunno why. Offered him one earlier, he tried n did not like. But still stole the chip with the most seasoning. Was really looking forward to that chip.

◆ ◆ ◆

I haven't made entries for the last few days. There are so many projects going on that I've been super tired by the end of the day. Benji has been wonderful as usual. Not happy with all of the machines moving around outside – lots of screaming. Got his man cave underneath his sleeping cage cleaned out the other day. Had to close the door to his room while he was busy in the play space, then work reallyreallyreally fast sweeping the entirety of cave contents into a bag, and then replacing it all before B knew what was going on. And I had to keep talking to him loudly since the door to the room was closed. If I stopped talking, he would scream. I usually have Howy come down and play with him while I clean the man cave, but he wasn't available. I got it done on my own! I had luckily saved a lot of the things he'd been chewing on and I've been sweeping it up. Cleaned and dusted it all and stored it in a bag. So I just dumped all of that under there. That way, it looked the same, but was clean. B didn't go to bed until 10 tonight – no screaming beforehand. Just climbed up and went to sleep.

◆ ◆ ◆

Went down at 2. I was tired and sore. I pulled several muscles while moving wet piles of old hay with the pitchfork. Intense pain. Sitting on the floor was really difficult on me today. Each time I'd try to lay on my back to stretch out, B would come and stand on me. Normally I'm fine with that, but I was already in such pain, and his claws are wicked bad right now. I wish our vet was closer - it's an hour's drive each way to get B's nails filed down.

We didn't get to go outside. Too windy. The door to outside was open, so wind was causing the door to the stairs to move and make noise, which drew B's attention. He rolled his barbell to the bumping door, stood it up on its end, placed his beak on the door, and made the weight clunk against the door a few times. Then he pushed the barbell against the door and left it there. The door stopped making noise. Hilarious.

I have to admit that I ended the day just a wee bit early. 430 instead of 5. He was tired, and getting a bit cranky. He usually poos from one of the shelving units when we play at his box. But he climbed up on me, and pooped on my back. It happens on ocassion and doesn't bother me, but on this day, that was sort of "it" for me. Apparently, I too was tired and getting a bit cranky. It was a combination of the pain I was in, his claws digging into me mercilessly, his wanting to climb on me constantly, and then pooping on me... I dunno. I think being in pain made me a bit more sensitive than usual, so I found being pooped on insulting, even though I knew full well it was not. But I put him to bed early. He was fine with it. Just went into his man cave with nary a peep of complaint.

◆ ◆ ◆

He actually cut our play time short today, by going into his room and hanging out under his cage. While I was prepping his room for the night he came out a lot and requested kisses. At one point, he stood in front of me, putting his beak up for a kiss, and each time I'd kiss it, he'd put it back up for another, and say, "Pretty bird." I think we were up to like 8 kisses before he went back to his man cave for the night. Damn he's adorable.

◆ ◆ ◆

I haven't had a chance to do daily entries. Sadly B-time rolls into horse dinner time, then our dinner time, and then crash time. I usually write during crash time, but I haven't been sleeping well, so crash time is very quiet in both mind and body. It was a very nice 3 days though.

I think it might have been Monday when we wrapped up the night a bit early because he was screaming a lot. He gave me no issue when I pulled the plug and closed up at 445. But our visits throughout the day were all fun.

A new game evolved recently, wherein he throws a plunger to me, I catch it, and throw it back. We played that for a long time, while he was perched on the shelves.

These little sink plungers are wonderful 'too toys. If Benji hadn't shown such an interest in the plunger in our bathroom, I'd never have thought of these as a toy. He is drawn to them so strongly that I cannot take him into a bathroom without first hiding the plunger. And I like that these mini ones (used for sink plunging) can be purchased in quantity for so little money. He loves them as a plunger, as a stick alone, and as the rubber plunger head alone. Each separate entity requires a different manner of play. Three toys in one.

I have noticed that Benji responds with a "yes" head nod when I ask him questions. And if his response is negative, he just doesn't nod, looks away, or walks off in another direction. Like if he's sitting on my shoulder and I ask if he wants to go outside, he answers with a nod. If he doesn't, he doesn't nod. If he does, he nods. Well, it's more of a bounce. It sounds nuts, but I swear he knows what I'm saying sometimes.

Tonight I told him, "Let's go eat some corn," and he went immediately to his dish of corn and waited for me to hand feed him.

◆ ◆ ◆

It's wet and cold outside, so we stayed in. As I was tearing apart some bread for the outside birds, he came over and took a hot dog bun. He nibbled on it for a minute, then ran off to the big box that he loves to play in, and pulled out the plunger – the full one, stick and all. He brought it to me, so I tossed it back in the box. He ran in and got it, brought it back out, and I threw it in

again. This went on for a veeeeerrrrry long time. Almost the entire time I was down there. Sometimes he'd go into the box and wait for me to throw it, while other times he'd wait outside of the box and then go in after it after I'd thrown it.

At first, he was okay with my tearing up bread as we played. But then he started giving me dirty looks over it. I was totally responsive to him each time he brought the plunger to me, but he did not like that I was distracted at all. He would come out with the plunger, I would cheer him on, he'd throw the plunger to me and then turn with an expression on his face that if verbalized, would be, "harrumph." Then he'd go back into the box and wait for me to throw the plunger in to him – though somewhat half-heartedly. So even though I'd do what I was supposed to do with no hesitation, he still didn't like the interference of the bread. So I stopped. And he was very happy. He'd bring the plunger closer to me, not give me dirty looks, and run instead of walk, back into the box. He was more "into it" when my attention was solely on him. It was pretty funny. And kind of demanding.

When I wanted him to take a nap because he was getting clumsy, I opened his playroom door and tossed his weight in. Almost always works. Normally, he runs in, I tell him I love him and he should have good sleepies, and then I close the door. But today he stopped short of the door ledge again. I videotaped it. He talked and talked, and would only finally go into the room when I went in. I closed the door behind me, he talked to me a lot, stood on my foot, talked some more, bit the phone when I sat down, and when I eventually walked out the door, he walked right with me. Such a cutie. He did go right back into the playroom though, and I left him to take a nap.

◆ ◆ ◆

Benji's breathing sounded stuffed up. While looking for information on bird colds I found an interesting site that lists the best air purifiers for bird owners. Some info on breeder's lung:

Although Bird Breeder's Lung is the most common version of hypersensitivity pneumonitis, it is not a problem for most bird owners. For some bird owners, however, repeated exposure to proteins found in bird dust, feather particles, or droppings can cause serious damage to lungs. The situation is more likely to occur when many birds are kept in a confined space and exposure is intense and/or over a prolonged period of time.

I found this very interesting: Birds have an incredibly efficient respiratory system, which can be both a blessing and a curse. Even though their air passages are small, these tubes are highly efficient in transporting air. However, because the airways are so tiny, they can quickly and easily become clogged.

When birds are forced to breathe air that is thick with dander and dust, as well as other normal household pollutants, it almost always leads to disease and infection which can shorten your bird's lifespan considerably.

Instinct allows birds to be able to effectively hide symptoms when they are ill. This behavior doesn't stop once they become a part of your family. Being able to hide the problem from their humans allows the illness to progress, until there is little or no chance of having them recover even with medical attention.

Above information from https://www.petassure.com/new-newsletters/controlling-bird-dust-and-dander/

Best air purifiers: Austin Air, IQAir and Airpura. Prices range from $599-$1299

We were outside for a shorter time than I'd have liked. He got down off my shoulder after maybe 10 minutes, and headed inside. I followed. We played in there – something like 2.5 hours of my throwing things, mostly a plunger, into the box where he was waiting. He'd bring it back to me, and then run into the box and wait for the next toss. There were smoothie breaks, snuggle breaks, and occasional changes of tossed item, including his weight, and a very chewed up plunger top. But mostly it was his full plunger. Very little snuggling, and when it happened it was for short periods of time. Like little snuggle bursts. By 4:00 he was getting a little cranky, and nipped my toe. So I put him into his room for a nap, and I went upstairs. I watched him on the monitor and he never slept. Just played. So at 415 I went back down and stayed with him til 515. Then I had to go feed horses, who were waiting impatiently because I was fifteen minutes late.

Couple of notables: When he's in a self-proclaimed time out from play, he turns the barbell upright to mark that it is no longer in play. When he's ready to play again, he turns it back on its side. Yesterday he did the same with the plunger for the first time. He brought me the plunger, and as I held it and waited for him to go back to the box, he stood there, looking at me, and then held out his foot. So I handed him the plunger, sliding the stick under his foot. He took it, and stood it upright. It rocked a bit, so he held his foot back up near it, steadying it. When it stopped rocking, he put his foot down, and walked over to his glass of smoothie. He drank and drank. When he was done, he walked back over to the plunger, knocked it on its side, and ran into the box. We're back in play.

◆ ◆ ◆

When I went down after yet another un-used Benji nap break, we went outside. The wind had died down, so I wanted him to get some more sun and warmth. He didn't want to go out, and he wouldn't come up on my hand. I had to convince him to head outside with me so he could get his sun requirement. I grabbed the plunger and swung it around to show him I had it. I skittered to the door and he ran after me. I ran outside, and he stopped while still inside. He ran around near the door, refusing to go out. I walked over to the sunlight space, sat down, and tossed the plunger in the air a few times. He was peeking out the door, sort of leaning from behind the wall so he could see me. He finally stepped out and slowly walked toward me. Once he got to me he climbed up on my shoulder. We sat for a few minutes, and then I put him up on the round pen. He meandered around up there for a few minutes. Howy was working in the paddock, and the horses were in the

stalls. Zalika came out of her stall to keep an eye on Benji. She doesn't trust
him. Eli joined her, and they both stood at the gate staring at Benjamin.
After a couple of minutes the two of them walked over to Howy and asked
him if he had any treats. He got some horsey love, and then they headed into
the pasture. Benji was quiet, so Zalika was not as concerned about his
presence.

◆ ◆ ◆

When we went inside, we played, and then I laid down on my side. He came
out of his box and started playing with my feet. I thought he was going to
bite them – which he did, but not in the usual prankish kind of way. I looked
down and then sat up, realizing he was trying to lay on my foot. He does that
with my hands, and with my arms when I cross them on my chest. He
straddles them, nips at them in the process of getting comfortable, and then
hunkers down and takes a nap, or at least just lays there very still and quiet.

When he couldn't get comfy on my foot he walked over and climbed up on
the couch. I followed. He waited for me, standing on the back of the
couch. I sat down, and put my arm on the pillow. He immediately ran –
seriously, he ran – and laid down on my arm/hand. We sat like that for
probably 20 min. Then he got up and rearranged himself by first leaving and
climbing onto the arm of the couch, then coming back and getting comfy
again. Maybe another 10 min of snuggles on my hand. He got up again, and
I got up, as I wanted to put the blueberries away in the basement freezer. He
came with me. He likes to stand on my shoulder and look inside the freezer.

Benji and I went outside one more time, walked around a bit, I pulled some
weeds, and then he wanted to go back in. So of course, we did. He ran into
his room, so I went in and swept up a few things on the floor, and replaced
his newspapers. While I did that, he did his usual "I don't want you to clean
so I'm going to stand in front of you and talk to you with much wing
emphasis and just generally look adorable so you'll kiss me" thing. It
worked.

We played some more, but then he snuggled and kept yawning, so at 315 I
put him down for a nap.

The later afternoon wasn't as enjoyable. Very nice, as always, but he was a little "off." He hadn't napped. I went back down at 4, and we played, went outside, etc., and did so until 515. Neighbor was coming over at 530 so I left B at 515 for that reason, and because he was getting crankier and yawning a lot.

◆ ◆ ◆

Overall, B was in a bad mood. Kind of a weird mood. He seemed grumpy at first – very grumpy. He was playing the plunger and box game, but with little enthusiasm, and a bit of attitude. He'd attack the plunger like a hawk attacking a rabbit. He'd throw it *at* me instead of to me, and then turn and walk slowly back to his box, in a rather deliberate, almost menacing manner, like he was trying to prove something - like Henery Hawk from the old cartoons. Other times he'd throw the plunger and then just stand there and stare at me. Twice he just stared off into space, and I had to say, "Are you ready?" for him to jerk back to reality and go into the box. It was weird.

He did drink a good amount of smoothie, which made me happy. After about an hour he calmed a bit, snuggled with me, and then played with more enthusiasm. Then he'd go off and wander around as if he was looking for something to do, but was uninterested in everything around him. Admittedly I've had those days too.

I tried to change things up and tossed the plunger in a new space instead of into the box. The first time I did it, he ran after it. The second time I tried that, he looked at me like I was an idiot who did not know enough to play by the rules he had set. He does not appreciate rebellion in his subjects. He did not go get it that time. In the last 30 minutes he yawned a few times, so I put him in his room at 4 and told him to take a nap. He did not nap.

I checked on him at 430. He had been sitting on the perch on top of his cage, looking like he might nap, but he was talking incessantly, and sometimes screaming. So I just went down and played with him again. He was a little better. We played until around 500. Then he went off to bite on the tall boxes, which he did for 10 minutes. When he tired of that, he began chewing on the corner of the wall. Left 6 huge gauges in it. I put him into his room, and left him for the night. He was okay with that.

Watching him on the monitor, sometime between 630 and 7 he climbed up on his cage, screaming and flapping his wings. It was what he normally does before bed, but he doesn't go to bed until sometime between 8 and 10 – later now that it's still light out at 8. So I don't know what fueled that event. It was the only time he did it tonight. He doesn't carry on each night however – just some. Perhaps he just went to bed early.

It's amusing and educational to watch him on the baby monitor. Sometimes he's very quiet and still, while other nights he is just so busy. He walks back and forth a lot, moving things from one place to another. He chatters away while looking through his toy boxes. Oftentimes he is playing with his weight. Then he'll take the weight to whichever man cave he's going to hang out in, set the weight on end, and go into the cave. He's very fastidious about it, making sure that it's upright and stable. It is the official position for "time out," or "weight not in play."

The other day, I was playing music off of my computer. A particular song came on, Glitter and Gold by Barns Courtney. He had an intense reaction to the song. And it was immediate. I don't know if he really really liked it, or if he hated it, but my guess by his reaction is it was the latter. He stopped dead in his tracks when the song came on in the playlist, and he stared at the computer. He looked at me a few times, his neck craned, his body tight. Then he climbed onto my shoulder, and hunkered down to do the squatting wing flapping dance while screaming. I turned the song off, and put on mellow piano music. He got off my shoulder and went back to playing. I'm going to try the song one more time to see if he has the same reaction. (I tried the song again the next day and he was fine with it, so I have no idea what that was about.)

Ordered one of the recommended air filters. The Austin Air Heavy Duty 700 sq ft air purifier. We'll see... (Note a month later – it sadly wasn't impressive)

◆ ◆ ◆

Finally got down to see Benji in the morning. He was so happy to see me. Made it down at 910. He came out of the "under-shelf" man cave, wings going, hopping around in happiness. I gave him a kiss, and then changed out his water while he was under his cage sorting through his toys. He came out with his weight and threw it. Then again. And again, until it was outside the room. I picked up his messy newspapers and threw them away. He was running around in the basement with his weight, and then he threw it back into his room. I picked it up, and tossed it back out, and joined him in the play space.

We played a lot, and he wandered a bit. He stood on his ladder chewing on bubble wrap, then went to the floor and chewed on some more.

We played again, he ran around a bit. I picked up his weight and held it in my hand, and ran around while he chased me. We just did a few laps, then it was back to the box game. At 1010 I put him down for a nap, which he did well and quietly, though he didn't actually nap until around noon, and that was full of talking bursts.

He did not like the day's smoothie, and barely had any at all. I put in more than the usual half of a lemon, so note that he isn't crazy about additional lemon in smoothies.

As we were wrapping up the night, I was sweeping the play space, and he was running around with me. I said, "Where is your weight?" because I had to have it to put back in his room. He walked into the box, shuffled around a bit, and then rolled it out of the box and announced, "Here!" Amazing. When I was ready to leave, he talked and talked and talked, as he does. It's so hard to leave him...

◆ ◆ ◆

Didn't make it down until 1030. We had a lovely time. Mostly just played the box game and snuggled. He switched a lot between the full plunger, roll of tape, plunger head, and barbell. At one point, he was in the box, with all of them. I said, "So what's going to be next?" He popped out, all fluffed up, and spread his wings a bit, as if he was saying, "Me!"

I left him to rest at 11:45, and went back down at 330. Later than planned. He was excited to see me. Climbed on my shoulder. I picked up the weight, and we headed out to the play space. I set him down and went back in to do some cleaning in his room. He ran back and forth thru the door trying to get me out to the play space. I joined him. We played, as always, but I put a movie on instead of music. I'm not going to say he didn't like it, but he didn't seem as "carefree" as he does with the music.

I had to feed the horses so left him at 445 to take care of that, and was back in his room at 530. It was slightly sunny, warm, and a calm day, so I took him outside. He excitedly jumped up onto the round pen, and sunned himself. He wandered now and again, sliding his way around on the rails. I stayed with him, just walking along the fence, or resting my chin on my arms on the fence near him. The Grackles were surrounding us, squawking like crazy. I thought it would bother B, but it did not.

I wanted to check out a bush in our garden that Howy said was a lilac bush. So I walked over to it, which is maybe 30 or 40 feet from the round pen. I worried B would scream, but he didn't. And it was. I noticed then that we had some HUGE stalks of asparagus there. I had forgotten about them. I picked a couple, and walked back to Benji. He put his foot out, requesting a stalk. I gave it to him. He picked it apart. I don't think he ate any of it, but he did chew it to pieces. And then he requested a second.

When the bugs had annoyed me to the point of wanting to go inside, he did not want to. I tried to get him onto my hand, but no. I tried to slide my fingers under his feet. He just spread them oddly in order to avoid my fingers. It looked humorous. I finally just walked into the basement. He screamed over and over and over... I got things ready for his bedtime while he screamed. As he screamed, he moved closer to the end of the roundpen rails. Once his room was ready for bedtime, I went out to get him, and he finally climbed onto my hand. I took him inside and put him to bed. I missed him the minute I closed the door. Weird how I always do.

I went down at 10:10, and we went outside almost immediately. Had a wonderful time. Walked the round pen, went to the front yard, hung out on the porch and retaining wall. While on the round pen, Howy came around the far corner of the house on the Dixie Chopper. He needed me to open the gate so he could mow the pastures. I ran up and did that. B screamed the whole time I was gone - which was all of maybe 15 seconds. Calmed once I was back. Oddly didn't scream because of the Dixie Chopper. He always screams at loud mechanical equipment. I wonder if he's getting used to it now.

Fed Ex delivered the new Austin Air air filter while we were outside. The

Fed Ex guy got a kick out of Benji. B conversed with him, and then laughed when I told the FE guy that the air filter was needed because of him (him being B, not FE guy). We went back down to the basement, and I was picking up newspapers and wiping down the floor. B kept bringing me his weight, and I would stop what I was doing and toss it for him. Then he tossed it to me, I grabbed it, and so did he. Again. Same finger, same location of wound, bleeding profusely and hurt like hell. I closed him in his room – he screamed – I went upstairs and tried to clean it and put on a band-aid. Can't get one on – bite covers too much of finger (top of beak and bottom of beak = whole finger wound) the sticky parts wound up on some part of the wound, no matter where I put it. So I wrapped it in a wet wipe and sat down on the couch with an ice pack on it. Man, this one seems to hurt more than usual. Throbbing and stinging at same time. Oh well, B got a good hour of outside time and sunlight, and that makes for a good morning.

Headed back down at 3 and stayed til 5. It's difficult for me to type – can't bend my finger. Nice afternoon. We played, then went outside again. Then played and rearranged the basement a bit. Put him to bed at 5, and as always, I missed him right away.

◆ ◆ ◆

Outside for awhile. Usual play. Went inside. Cleared the room by moving things around so there's more open space. He enjoyed the result, running after the weight for long distances. Went into his room to put down his papers and he brought the weight in there, throwing it at me. I tossed it for him, and we played in there for awhile. Then he walked by and bit my toe. No idea why. He just did. Frustrated me since I was already nursing a huge swollen and painful finger from his bite. He's getting bitey. I don't like it. Perhaps I need to initiate time-outs when he does that. Finger bites are always an accident so no punishment is warranted. But the toe nips – those are intentional. Not having had that thought about time outs when the nip happened, we kept playing, and when I was done cleaning we went out to the play space. I threw the weight really far each time, trying to cut down on the number of times I had to throw it since it annoyed my finger. Eventually he grew winded. I told him he needed to chill a bit, and get his breath back. I put the weight on its side to signal a time out. He ran over and grabbed it with great force, threw it to the ground, and waited for me to throw it again.

Apparently only he can call time outs. As we played, he kept getting in the way as I'd try to pick up the weight, or when I'd try to throw it. I was constantly working around him and risking another finger bite. I realized this was going nowhere good, and put him back in his room so he could calm down. Went upstairs to get ready for the horses' vet and ferrier appointments.

When I got back into the house after the appointments, he was screaming. I turned on the baby monitor music and he stopped.

Went back down at 4 and stayed til 6. We went outside at first, and I sat us down over by the barrier wall to block the wind. He sat on my shoulder quietly for awhile, and just looked around at the birds all over the yard. Then he climbed down and waddled over to the round pen and climbed up. He had a slight tumble as he climbed, flapping wings... and I happened to be videotaping. I turned it off and ran over, but he had already righted himself and gotten up just fine – as I knew he would. I stayed there with him, and he wandered a wee bit. Then he looked over the edge at me, which I know is him saying he's ready to come down. I put my hand up, and he climbed into my arms where he stayed for a long time. He likes that on windy days. He still gets sun, but I turn my body so that he's blocked from the wind.

We went inside at his request. We played in there, mostly in his room with the door open. I don't know why – he just seemed to want to be in there. I wanted some time to look his room over and plan where to put the new air cleaner, so I didn't mind at all. He didn't bite me, which was great. We stayed in there with only occasional voyages outside of the room – mostly for me to look for parts to build the protection gear for the new air cleaner. I had hoped to put it inside his cage, but this Austin cleaner is too big for that. It's a conundrum.

The horses have open stalls, which means they go into them at their will. They use them for naps and meals, and to escape the sun and weather elements. I can see them from the basement window, so at 6:00 when I saw all three were in their stalls, looking out the windows, I knew they were ready for dinner. I told Benji I had to go feed the horses. He broke out into a boisterous conversation, wouldn't let me close his door, wouldn't stay in his room – made me chuckle and sad that I couldn't stay longer. I promised him I would see him in the morning. He allowed me to leave, and he happily hunkered down in his man cave.

◆ ◆ ◆

Went down from 9-10. He was super snuggly. We spent almost all of the time outside. I took down a pail of soil I had dug up from the pasture – we had needed a soil sample. Howy suggested I let Benji empty it into the garden area. B loved that. Spent a good amount of time pulling it out of the pail in clumps and setting it in the grass. We didn't take it to the garden because he didn't really want to be that far from the door for some reason. After snuggling, and spending some time on my shoulder, he got down and walked back inside. I love it when he does that. Just waddles on over and waits at the door. If it's open, he'll go right on in. But when it's closed, he just stands and waits while peering in the windows.

I went back down again at 2, and stayed til 5. We played the usual games, he spent time in the tall cardboard box, chewing on the sides, and let me get a few cleaning things done. We're having the stove down there taken away in a day or two, so I need to make sure that there is a pathway. We played in his room, listened to music, and just generally hung out. He did a lot of talking in his room. He talks more in there than anywhere else. Interesting. I guess it's where he's most comfortable. Or maybe, since it's his home, he feels as host it's his responsibility to keep the conversation going.

At 5 I went out to feed the horses, clean the stalls, and fill the hay bowl. Got back to Benji at 530, and stayed til 6ish. In that last half hour we mostly played in his room, talked a lot, just hung out. He came out of the room, pulled a few toys out of the metal pail, and threw them around. As I was sitting in the doorway of his room, I noticed the little toy recorder that had fallen behind the doll house. I pulled it out and started playing it – very, very badly. But he loved it! He bounced around and danced and danced. Then he started singing. How cute is that??

He was very good about my leaving. He did run out of the room when he realized what was happening, but went right back in, and I closed the door and turned on his music. He just went back to playing.

◆ ◆ ◆

Benji-time was a bit later than I wanted. I had to do some cleaning in the kitchen in preparation for the new stove delivery. I got down to him around

1030. We hung out until noon. He was hyper, and random. He'd go from one toy to another to another to snuggling to playing with one toy then another then another... and he screamed frequently. I had to finish clearing the path so the guys could take the stove from the basement – the one the previous owners left. B didn't like that. Not at all. Some days he doesn't mind, as long as I'm quick about it. This was not one of them. He SCREAMED. Good times.

At one point, I sat down on the sofa and he joined me and snuggled on my arm. His few minutes of quiet.

I went down again at 2, and stayed until 4, then went back down at 6 and stayed til 640. The first time was about the same as the morning visit. The short evening visit was nice though. Went outside for awhile, then went into his room and hung out there until I put him to bed. He talked a lot when I stood to leave, but he quieted quickly. He really just wanted to chew on things.

I went down at 1030 and took Benji outside. We walked around to the front of the house where I thought he would play with the weight on the driveway. He did not. He wandered away from me and stood on the driveway screaming. Don't know why. His cheek feathers were forward, so he was indicating happiness. The screams seemed loud for happy. Then again, volume really has no bearing on emotion, unless he's super, *super* pissed. That's a loud I cannot handle.

We hung out on the driveway with him wandering and me sitting down by the windbreak created by Howy's truck. I kept an eye on him mostly by looking under the truck. It can be difficult to keep him from going under the vehicles, and I wanted to make sure he didn't... I know nothing about cars, but fear that with one chomp we could be without brakes.

At one point he disappeared from view. I walked over to find him. I sat down near him and he climbed onto my arm, facing my chest, and snuggled for so long that my back started to hurt. He cooed and said quiet pretty babies... I sat so I was his windbreak.

When my back couldn't take it anymore, I stood up and we walked to the porch to sit on the bench. I put him on it and then pulled the bench out slowly so it was in the sun. I wanted him to get his sun for the day. We hung out there, played with his weight on the porch, chewed on some grass... Howy came out and sat with us for awhile. He and Benji played with the weight a few times. When Howy went back inside, B and I stayed out for a few more minutes but I got pretty hot. We went inside and played with the weight until I headed up for lunch.

I went back down at 3 and stayed til 510. I didn't want to leave him, but had to feed the horses. In that time, we played inside and out. We were outside for a very short time. I just couldn't convince him to spend much time out there. Inside we mostly played with his big round weight rather than the 1.5lb. He hasn't played with that bigger one in quite awhile. The last few days he's been turning to things he hasn't played with in a long time, as well as things he's never shown an interest in - pulling out old toys, as well as new items I've brought down from upstairs, or got from St. Vinny's in the last few days.

I went back down at 6. When I got inside his room I saw that he had 2 things stuck to his feet. It was adorable. One was a piece of tape (he had dissected a roll of masking tape between my visits) and the other was a piece of that thin paper styrofoam-like stuff used for packing stereos and whatnot. He wandered around with those stuck to his feet for a minute or two. It didn't bother him, and it made me laugh. When I realized they weren't going to fall off themselves, I took them off of him. We went outside, and Sherri drove by in her Gator. She pulled up into the driveway and marveled at the adorable bird on my shoulder. He stayed with us for a short while, but was fidgety and nervous due to her dogs. So I put him up on the porch bench and went back to chat with Sherri. Howy joined us. He hadn't had the chance to meet Sherri yet, so that was nice. Benji walked around on the bench and made his blender noise the entire time. Right before Sherri left, he did a bit of singing.

B and I went back to the basement. I was going to stay outside with him, but the tiny bugs kept swarming us and it was truly annoying. Plus, there was a fly that kept dive-bombing Benji and he abhores that.

I convinced B to come outside by sitting out there. He'd roll the weight to me, and I'd roll it back inside the basement through the open door. After awhile I rolled it onto the sidewalk outside the basement. He ran out for it. Once through the door, he looked around and found all sorts of things to interest him, including the bucket of dirt, which he pretty much emptied. I tried to get him away from the house by walking around. He followed me for a bit, and then I turned to see him just standing watching me, while flicking his head around. He was being attacked by bugs. He turned to go back to the basement, and I followed, swatting bugs along the way. Weird how they can suddenly just be there...

At one point while playing inside, I was sitting in his room with him, writing something down, and had my leg extended while sitting on the floor. I wasn't paying attention to him for, oh, maybe 7 seconds. I could see him out of my peripheral vision, but was looking at the paper on which I was writing. He was just standing there staring at me. And then he bit my toe. Hard enough to hurt and shock me, but not hard enough to break the skin. I wanted to get up, leave, and close the door so he knew he was being bad, and I wasn't going to stick around if he was going to bite me. But I also had things in his room I couldn't leave in there. By the time I stood up and picked up all my stuff and stormed off, he'd not learn a thing. He'd just think I was leaving – in a rude fashion no less. My guess is, like horses, if you don't discipline immediately, you lose your window and they don't know for what they're being disciplined. Then all it does is confuse, and potentially anger them, causing a rift in the relationship. Consequently, B immediately got a disciplinary, "Ouch! Don't do that!" But no time out.

Left him for lunch, and went back around 2. We played inside the entire time. Bugs were getting worse, as they do later in the day. He has a new way to move the big red weight – end over end. He picks it up by the tape on one end, stands it on end, then pushes it over. Then he does it all over again – again and again. Such talent he has.

He also has to pull the tape off of that barbell. He yanks a chunk off before he throws it almost every single time. And he loves to dart out from under his cage and sort of attack the weight – something out of the norm for him. He hides under his cage, I roll the weight, and he flies out like a rocket to get it before it lands at its final location. He grabs it with force from the tape on the side of an end. He's a real brute with this thing...

He also stood close to me and rolled it gently to me, then waited for me to gently roll it back to him. For this he uses his feet, not his beak. It's very cute. I love watching him grab things with his feet. Which reminds me, last night I opened up the big container of sunflower seeds for him. Well, wait, I didn't, he did. I took it to him and he opened it, tossed the lid aside, and stood there eating right out of the bucket. Then he put his foot out for me to pick him up, so I slid my hand under his foot. He climbed on and used me as a stepping stool so he could easily get to the top of the bucket and stand on the rim. While doing so, he ate with his foot instead. He'd pick up a big footful, bring it to his mouth, and eat the footful of seeds over the course of a few seconds. Then he would dig down deep for another footful. It's messy, but adorable.

◆ ◆ ◆

While playing in his room, he ran by me as I was moving my hand to get the weight, and my finger brushed past his eye. He said, "Ow, you hurt me," and ran under his cage. I got him to come back out, gave him some kisses and apologized. All was forgiven. How does he know to say these things?

◆ ◆ ◆

He barely snuggled today. It was a day all about play. I missed his snuggles. I told him so. He was heading after the weight, then sort of stopped, and I said "I sure do miss your snuggles... " He turned and stood there looking at me. I put on a sad face. I still can't believe this happened... he walked over to me, climbed onto my lap, and snuggled with me! It wasn't for long, but it was a snuggle! Was at least a 4 minute snug. He is so smart. I don't think I can even tell anyone that happened because they'll think I'm making it up.

The other funny thing was when he was playing really hard in the afternoon session, I finally told him he had to stop and have some smoothie before he could play any more. Earlier he had turned down the offered smoothie 3x in favor of playing. I really wanted him to just chill for a minute, so I said, "I'll throw the weight again after you've had some smoothie." He went over and drank some smoothie. Not a small amount either. When he finished, he ran to his box to wait for me to throw the weight – which I did.

◆ ◆ ◆

We played with the round weight the hour I was there. I got him to join me outside, but only from the doorway. He'd roll the weight to the door, and then wait for me to roll it back into the basement. Near the end of the hour he did come out and sit on my lap for a few minutes. It was another charity cuddle prompted by my saying how much I missed his snuggles.

I have been trying to teach him to climb onto my shoulder "on command." It's not going well so far. Doesn't surprise me. He likes commands about as much as I do.

At one point we were playing with his barbell, and he needed to take a break and munch on some black oil sunflower seeds. He brought the barbell and set it next to me, using his beak to set it on its side. He looked at me, reached over with his foot, touched the barbell and said, "Leave it." He had some sunflower seeds, then ran back over, knocked the barbell onto its side, and was ready to play again.

◆ ◆ ◆

Again today, I had to stop playing with him at one point and told him that he had to have some smoothie before we played anymore. I needed him to take a break, as he was panting from so much running around. He actually drank some smoothie, and then, I swear, he said, "Ok I drank some," and then he put the weight back flat on the floor and ran to the box so I could throw the weight to him. And I did.

Down again at 2. He was laid back, almost bored. And calm. Barely played. Mostly walked around looking at things, and hung out on the gate. He did climb onto my leg and sit there, fluffed and happy, shaking in happiness a little bit, for a very long time. We hung out and played until 345 and then I headed outside to move manure. Good times. Back in his playroom at 5, and stayed until 6. He was "on" the entire time. Dancing, shaking his head, hopping around, singing... Drank a lot of smoothie. And we played with the big round weight a lot.

When I went into his room to turn off the new air purifier, he followed me in. I closed the door after I grabbed his metal weight. He climbed onto the side of the cage and he talked and talked and talked and talked. I sat and

listened, nodded, and responded now and again. He was cute as a bug's ear.
I always hate to say good-bye. I really wish he'd be happy and not screamy
and destructive upstairs. It's difficult to spend so much time in the basement,
but also, it inhibits how much time I can be with him. Weirdly, I seem to be
more affected by it than he is. I'm trying to set up the basement so it will be
easier on me, and I would *love* it if I could get it, and keep it, much
cleaner. But the bottom line is that the concentrated Benji time means I can't
really do much else, at least not with any precision or thoroughness. Can't
work on the computer while he plays. Can't vacuum up all of the tiny plastic
bits hiding underneath things - he hates the noise of a vacuum. Can't dust all
of his toys - so I do them in shifts, which means by the time I finish the last
bunch, it's time to go back and do the first batch again. Can't text or look at
my phone. Can't even just sit and stare out the window. He demands me in
my entirety. I get it – I'm only there for 3 hours in total and that leaves him
21 hours to be alone. He deserves all my attention. And I love giving it to
him. So what am I complaining about??

◆ ◆ ◆

When I went down at 520 I got quite a giggle. Sadly I was unable to get this
on video. I was sitting on the floor cleaning up his "spent cartridges"
(sunflower seed shells). He came out from under his cage to roll the weight
to me, and when I looked up and saw him I broke out laughing. He had tufts
of pillow stuffing on the top of each foot, so it looked like he was wearing
little elf shoes. It was adorable. They fell off after only a few steps.

There was a period in the afternoon visit where he was acting very bored.
He'd walk up to the tape, toss it once, then go to the weight, push it a few
inches, go to the other weight, push it, pick up a lid, toss it, pick up another
lid, chew on it and then toss it. Just so bored... As Howy said, "Just more of
the same."

◆ ◆ ◆

Someone was an absolute bug today. When I arrived, he said "Hi Baby" as
he usually does. I set his food down, and he went outside the room.
Normally he has been staying inside, but he wanted to play in the play space
today, which was nice. We played for a very short time, and then he climbed
onto my shoulder, and we went outside. I put him on the round pen fence,

and he wandered around on it. When he got to the middle, he stopped, and just sat there. Quietly. Soaking up the sun. I kicked off my shoes, pulled up my pant legs, and laid down on the bench. We were both just hanging out quietly, the only sounds around us were birds and horses. It was lovely. Hot, but lovely. After, I dunno, maybe 15 minutes, he sauntered on over to where I was laying on the bench, perched high up on the top bar of the round pen fence. I looked up and he was directly above me. I said hello to him. He put his foot out. I sat up and offered him my arm. I laid back down and he snuggled on top of me for a long time. Easily 20 minutes. Then he got back on the fence and hung out there again for a bit. Had a screaming session. Weird how anything that happens in our yard echos. The echo of Benji's scream is a much higher pitch than his actual scream.

He got down and walked around in the grass a bit, then came over to me as I was still on the bench. I offered him my foot, and he climbed on. The foot elevator brought him up to the bench seat. I offered him some smoothie, and he very happily ingested a LOT. He drank steadily for a long time. While he was drinking, I was starting to feel the effects of the sun and wanted to head inside. As soon as he was done drinking, I put the lid on the smoothie, gathered up my stuff, and offered him my hand. He jumped on, and inside we went.

Once inside, we played with all sorts of toys, all on the oceanscape mat. He didn't try to eat anyone's eyes today. Howy had re-wrapped his barbell in tape – just the ends. Benji loved that. He ran, danced, sat on my leg, sung, hopped, played with various toys... It's almost 10pm as I type this, and I can hear him down there rolling the weight around right now.

When we went into his room to play at one point, he would roll things to me, and then run to his bowl and grab a few pieces of food, or a nut, and eat it while talking to me. I just love it when he does that. Most of the time he would grab the food in his beak, then dunk his beak in the water, run to a spot near me, then take the food into his foot and hold it while munching on it. And talking. Always talking.

Because he was being so good, and in such a good mood, I decided to see if perhaps he would let me lay down some of the gym mats. They've been sitting in the basement in a box for maybe 2 weeks – perhaps longer. Today was the day I'd try get them down without angering the Little Price.

He was fine with it! I had to sweep first, and do some rearranging of items so that I could lay them down. He followed me around and rolled the weight to me while I did these things, and as long as I commented, and rolled the weight back to him, he was more than happy. He enjoyed running on the mats once they were down, chasing me as I'd go get more mats, and helping me unwrap them. Overall, he just had fun, and I had a really good day.

◆ ◆ ◆

I went down at 2, and we went outside for a short while. He walked back inside, so I followed. We played with various toys. Nothing seemed to truly intrigue him.

We snuggled on the couch for a long time. He hunkered down on my arms, wrapped his wings around them, and fell asleep for awhile – as did I. When he woke, we played a bit more, but then he saw the huge farm equipment working next door and had a fit. Screamed and screamed and screamed. So I put him in his room and closed the door. I left him alone until the harvesting was done. I went out and showered the horses.

When I went back down, we had more fun just playing, dancing, hopping... And snuggling. Lots of snuggling. We even snuggled on the couch again. He hunkered down, wrapped his wings around my arms and nestled quietly. When he got up, it was about 515 so it was dinner time for the horses. I left him in his room, and I went upstairs. When I got there, the horses were out in the pasture, and Howy said he'd handle dinner when they got back to the stalls. So I was able to return to Benji.

I opened his door and he was very happy to see me. He was dangling on the side of the cage, and he sort of danced up and down and said, "Hi Baby." He climbed down, and we played and snuggled until 630. When I left him, he was fine.

◆ ◆ ◆

We went outside for a short while in the early afternoon. Then later, we were out for an hour. I laid on the bench catching some rays, while B hopped around on the round pen. Later, he came over and sat with me, then left, then came back and laid on my arms, with his wings wrapped around my hands. To get to that position, using his foot, he moved my right hand, which was

petting him, and placed it on top of my left hand, then climbed on. I think
I'm going to seek out a stuffed animal for him. I wasn't going to, because he
will destroy it, and I'd feel badly for it. First, he'll pluck out its eyes, and then
he will pull out all the stuffing. But I really do think he needs something to
snuggle with when I'm not around. Maybe he won't obliterate it - who
knows?

We stayed outside until he was panting. But once I got him inside, he
wouldn't drink water or smoothie. Just wanted to play. So we played. I left
to feed the horses, and he was very good about it. I went back when I was
done, and we played and snuggled some more. He was good when I left –
talked a lot, but let me go without screaming. He was yawning when we
snuggled, so it didn't surprise me.

◆ ◆ ◆

Another lovely day. During phase one, we went outside pretty early on, but it
was soooo hot out we only stayed for about 15 minutes. We played inside,
and again he was sort of bored with all of his usual toys, and I couldn't get
him interested in some of the old toys he used to play with. I had gone to St
Vinny's this morning and gotten him some new things. So I brought out the
bag, and he went through it with his beak, but was mostly excited by the bag.
We played some more, and then went back outside. He climbed on the
geodome and I sat at the base of it. When he came down minutes later, he
climbed onto my shoulder, and we sat like that for awhile.

While we were playing, he did the cutest thing. He was throwing the large
perch around, and then he picked it up, and bonked himself lightly on the
beak a few times. Just like to do to him while drumming.

◆ ◆ ◆

Howy and I brought down 2 large empty boxes. I put the smaller of the two
on its side, down on the floor, in replacement of one I had Howy take away
because it was in such bad shape. The new box was apparently full of
intrigue... Benji had to pull the styrofoam out, and then play in
it. https://www.youtube.com/watch?v=TlldRAxfGRY

Eventually he took some of his favorite toys and ran those into the box to
play with them there. This was followed by tearing up sections of the floor

of the box. Then he played with all sorts of things, running them to me so I'd
roll or toss them into or near the box. He danced, and sang, and screamed
and snuggled. At one point, he came over to me and put his beak up, which
is his way of asking for a kiss. This is a move normally reserved only for
distracting me while I'm trying to clean. I was honored.

Benji was doing so many adorable things today, and talking a lot. Of course,
I didn't take the phone down with me to take any video. He's getting more
used to it, but he remains reserved when it's on – even when I don't hold it
myself – he knows... and he tones himself down.

Hilarious thing I want to report on that probably only Howy will believe... I
was sitting out in the play space, where we were playing with his barbell. B
suddenly walked away from me, toward his room, and he said "Be right
back." He went into his room, got a toy, and came back with it. He dropped
it in front of me, said something in Cockatoo-speak, and then ran to his
playbox. He uses phrases he hears me say, and he uses them correctly. It is
truly fascinating.

◆ ◆ ◆

He's saying things more clearly these days. We played, mostly in his room. I
sat outside his door, and rolled things into the room for him. He spent a lot of
time bringing me the cement half of the 2 pound weight he keeps pulling
apart. At one point, I reached over and got the other half of that weight, and
placed it in his room, right around the corner of the door. He walked over
and said, "I don't want it there." I said, "Ok, I'll move it then." I picked it up
and put it outside the door, and he nodded in a satisfied manner and turned
back to playing.

◆ ◆ ◆

His red weight was becoming dangerous. He had one half of it gone, and the
other remaining portion had a lot of sharp edges, which makes it a danger to
Benji. He gets the tape off more quickly every time. So I decided it was time
to throw that one away and bring in the next one. Hooooooboy was he a
happy bird!

The new barbell was on the other side of the basement – the side in which he
is not allowed until I get it set up for him. He was playing happily when I

went over there, but started wandering as I was heading back. I stepped over the barrier, and he saw me – and then he saw the new weight in my hand. He danced with such joy! He jumped around, walked ahead of me while looking back at me the whole time, and he was hopping and flapping his wings and chattering up a storm... I sat down, turned on the phone's video, and tossed the barbell for him. He rolled that weight around the basement for a good 15 minutes or more – just rolling, rolling, rolling, never stopping.

He ran around so much, I finally had to take it away from him. He was panting, but wouldn't slow down to catch his breath. I put the barbell on top of the toy box to force him to chill out, and all he did was try to get to it.

When he pooped off the gate, I noticed that the poo was foamy from all the running around – as if he had been shaken up like a can of soda. Interesting, and highly amusing.

He finally sat on my lap for awhile, and calmed down while getting pets. Then he was up again, and ready to go, so back to the toy box he went to indicate that he wanted the new barbell. I distracted him with a few other toys. I eventually got the weight down for him, and he played for a few minutes, and then started chewing on it, tearing a piece off. I was bummed. It didn't even last undamaged for a day. Not even an hour, actually. I tried to get him to just roll it, but he kept chewing on it post-roll. I put it back up on the toy box. I'll have Howy tape it up so maybe it will last a little bit longer if he has to chew through tape first.

My back started to hurt, so I laid down on my side, and rolled things to him from that position. After awhile he came over and snuggled up to my chest for a minute or two. Then he walked down to my feet and climbed up. He walked up my leg, stopping on my hip. He started playing with his chin feathers, sort of hunkered down in relaxation as he does, and looking around the room in his mellow manner. Suddenly his eye caught sight of the weight, which I had moved from the toybox to a new higher spot so he couldn't see it. Well, couldn't see it from the floor. But standing on my hip, he could. He stood straight up, on alert, jumped off my legs, ran to the box on which the barbell was placed, and danced, chattering away in excitement. Aye aye aye...

◆ ◆ ◆

I got a lot of video, so I'm not going to make a long entry. I do want to note that at one point I was cleaning up his grape skins, and I said, "Wow, you ate 3 grapes!" and he said, "I ate 3 grapes." It was so discernible. And of course, the phone wasn't recording. So I wanted to make sure I got it in the journal. I'm hoping my mind just placed the "I" in there because I can't believe he would know how to use pronouns.

◆ ◆ ◆

He's saying a lot of things, but I don't know what they are. It's frustrating. I can hear words, but cannot decipher exactly what he's saying, and he's not one to repeat himself. It's one of the reasons I'm doing these videos, but truth be told, he's a different bird with the camera on. You wouldn't think he'd understand that when the phone is propped up it's recording him. But he knows... Oh, he knows...

Since I was listening to some audio files on my phone this evening, I wasn't able to video him, and he liked that. He did find it very odd that my voice was coming out of the phone on the table, while I was sitting on the floor... He kept going up to it and staring at it, leaning his ear into it, and twice he picked it up and threw it.

◆ ◆ ◆

Benji was the picture of discontent. I don't know why. He didn't come out of his room for a good 10 minutes once I'd opened the door. That's never happened that I can recall. He's become a super sloppy pooper – spraying it all over the place. That's not part of the discontent thing – just a comment I thought of since the first thing I do after I open his door is clean up his poo (unless he climbs on my shoulder – then it's all about him). I sat outside in the play space waiting for him, and I broke up bread for the birds and ground squirrels. He finally came out, climbed up onto the gate, and shot out a super messy poo. We went outside early on. He roamed on the round pen gate panels, first walking around, preening, stretching and just generally hanging out. He snuggled a bit. Then he went off on a screaming spree. Constant. Loud. Abrasive. Unstoppable. And super annoying to the horses.

He didn't want to go inside, and would not step up when I offered my hand. He would just skitter on by, continuing his rampage. This went on for a very

long time, with occasional short breaks. The breaks were way shorter than
the rampages. I could see Zalika was glaring at us, while Ayesha and Eli
were watching B from their stall windows. I tried to calm him – not
happening. I went inside for awhile, did some basic cleaning, some
sweeping, swept his room and the play space. He was still screaming. I went
outside, and it didn't stop him. I stayed out for awhile, no change. I could
feel the red hot glares of the horses for my allowing him to interrupt their
serene surroundings. I went back in and got his barbell and stood in the
doorway with it. He stopped and stared. Then screamed some more. I
tossed the weight. He stopped, and then started again. I picked up the weight
and tossed it around. He stopped, then screamed again. I went over to see if
he wanted to come down to come play with the toy. Nope. That usually
works. Hmm... Since we were outside, and neighbors could potentially see
me, I was not going to dance, which almost always makes him stop
screaming. Nope, no one needs to see that...

I put the weight back inside, and went in to do some more cleaning - might as
well make use of the opportunity - and grab some items I needed to tear up so
I could replace all of the stuff under his cage. He continued to scream, and
scream. I went back out, and while screaming, he put his foot up. He was
finally ready to come in. We went in and he screamed some more inside.
We played for a short while and then it was time to feed the horses. Boy, it is
so true - when a U2 really wants to scream, there is no stopping it.

When I came back in from feeding the horses, I debated what to do. Benji
was quiet on his own, and screamy with me around. Should I go back down
and risk more screaming? Or should I leave him on his own since he's quiet?
After much deliberation, I decided to leave him on his own. A bold move. A
move that made me feel guilty every minute. But he's quiet. It's 620, and I
just checked him on the baby monitor. He was sitting on top of his cage,
napping. Minutes later he stretched. Then climbed down and went under his
cage. Not a peep. I swear that the monitor camera down there must light up
or something when I turn it on upstairs, because he always looks at it... Super
creepy.

So he's fine. And yet, I feel terrible.

It's now 9:00 as I make my journal entry, and he never made a peep. Must
have been having a "solo" day.

◆ ◆ ◆

Benji was standing on the back of my chair. I handed him the stick from his perch - the one he chewed so it no longer held him. He took it in his foot, and then dropped it. I picked it up and handed it to him again. He dropped it. He did this five times, looking me in the eye, and I laughed every time. I love watching him "drop the mic." When he decided that game was over, he looked at me and laughed, and dropped the mic one last time.

◆ ◆ ◆

I went down around 3. He came out right away, said "Hi Baby" and went to the play space. He made a scatter-poo, then got down off the gate and went to find a toy. We played a bit, mostly with the weight. Then he got screamy again. We played in his room for a bit, rolling the weight back and forth. I finally figured something out. While we were playing, I rolled the weight so it would go under his cage – but not hard enough to make it go deep under the cage (because of his egg). He got it, held it in his beak, and clucked at me. And I figured out that I think he's telling me not to roll it there at all – because his egg is there. It also dawned on me that if it has taken me this long to figure that out... yikes that's embarrassing. I also realized that he had his egg with him in his nest, which is probably why he's been so screamy. He wants to be out and about, but he also wants to be with his egg. So he's torn, and screamy. Ahhh yes, responsibility. 'Tis a heavy burden.

◆ ◆ ◆

Back downstairs, we played for maybe another 30-40 minutes. I got some video of him doing this weird thing he does, where he puts the weight upended, just at the edge of his reach. Then he stretches his leg out and grabs it with his foot. He puts his head on the ground, against his cage, or against a wall (or in one case, against my leg), and he pushes the weight around in circles, and then pushes it over until it falls. It's pretty strange. Looks like bird yoga. When I showed Howy the video of him doing this, Howy called it "downward facing cockatoo."

◆ ◆ ◆

A little after 7, Marcy and Emmie came over. Marcy was dropping off a key to their house so I could feed their fish and collect their mail while they're away next week. Emmie wanted to go see Benji, so we went downstairs, and I opened his door. He was in his man cave under his cage. He peeked out and said "Hi Baby." He came out, stepped into the doorway and saw two new people in his play space. I thought he might get a kick out of it – he loves an audience. He did not get a kick out of it. It bothered him. He fluffed up a little and stared at them. Without looking at me, he put his foot up so I'd put him on my shoulder. He did not stop staring at them. I reached down and got him, and put him on the gate. He faced the exterior doors and pooped, and then turned around and stared at them, and me, fluffed and shaking. Emmie moved forward to pet him, but I stopped her. I explained that he was apparently more nervous than I was expecting, so we should leave him be. I gave him about 30 seconds to see if he would calm down. When he didn't, I put him back in his room. Emmie looked in at him through the window in the door. He said a few things, and we left him. He went back to his egg.

I told Emmie if she saw us outside she should feel free to come over and see him, but tonight, because he's not used to having visitors at night, he was not himself.

So I don't know if it was the egg thing, or being seen when he's usually left alone, but he was off kilter. Altho, he was a bit off kilter throughout the afternoon, so... It's probably the egg. Then again, the few other times he had visitors post-bedtime, he was also not happy about it. He doesn't like being bothered once he's been put to bed. I get it - I'm the same way.

When I went down for the last visit of the day, he was super playful, and snuggly. Played with the smaller weight, and almost entirely out in the play space instead of his room. I tried to see if he would do anything if I were sad, by pretending to be sad when he moved away from one of my offered scrooches. I learned that he didn't really care if I was sad. And after awhile, he just screamed at me as I sat there with my head down wearing a sad face. He was happy again when I smiled and went back to playing with him as normal.

A lovely day. He did spend some time with his egg, but overall he seems to be back to normal. He played with many toys he's not looked at in awhile. He went outside with no issue, and roamed the round pen. He sat comfortably on the gate and preened. Benji was in good spirits during all of my visits today. He talked a lot. While we were inside, Howy was out mowing for the late afternoon/prevening portion of our time together, and normally B would scream bloody murder at that. But today, Howy found a way to remedy this - at least temporarily. B screamed the first few times Howy drove by the glass doors of the basement. Then Howy stopped the mower (didn't turn it off, just stopped moving) looked in the doors smiling, and waved at Benji. After that, B celebrated the fact that Howy was whizzing by on the mower by lifting his wings and singing each time Howy drove by. And I actually got it on video.

◆ ◆ ◆

While Benji and I were outside, we harvested some velvet leaf seed pods for our morning smoothies. I put them all into a pail as we were picking them. I fed B a few of the seeds, and he ate each one. When we had a good amount in the pail, we sat down on the bench, and I set the pail down alongside us. Benji climbed down off of my shoulder, reached his head into the pail, only to find he couldn't reach the pods. So he pulled the pail onto its side with his foot, and immediately began pulling out the pods and tossing them every which way. Hilarious.

I picked them all up and put them back in the pail, got B on my shoulder, and we headed inside. I set him on the gate, and put the pail on the floor. Told him to have at it, since inside they'd be much easier to pick up on the basement floor. He climbed down the gate, ran over, and definitely had at it. Seed pods everywhere.

◆ ◆ ◆

I was sitting outside the open door to his room, and we were rolling the weight around on his floor. I had to reach to get it at one point, and as I was reaching into the room I turned and looked under his cage. I broke out laughing. He has a second egg under there. There is now the ping pong ball, and a plastic egg. I looked behind the door at the container of the dozen plastic eggs. There was one missing.

He talked a lot, played with many various toys, and used the word "best" after I told him he was the best bird – which I tell him everyday.

He's such a joy. So often it's hard to believe he is a bird.   He's just so child-like. I told Howy that he'll know if I get Alzheimer's because Benjamin will start wearing clothes. I'm thinking of dressing him like an adorable little British child, with a little blazer, short pants and a Jaxson hat. I will tell everyone he is my son.

◆ ◆ ◆

He wanted some sunflower seeds, which were sitting in their container up on the toy box. He walked to the toy box, and looked up at the container. I got it down for him. He flipped the top off with his beak, and ate away. After a few minutes of chowing down, he was apparently thirsty. He walked back to the toy box, looked up at the bottle of water sitting on top of it, looked at me, and back at the bottle. I got it for him, opened it up, and poured it into his beak a few times. He drank a lot. Such a smart boy – he knows how to get what he wants.

I played the new chimes, and the new drum I bought the other day. He danced, complete with excellent head banging head swings. He's a very talented dancer. Of course, he does these adorable things when I don't have the phone with me...

◆ ◆ ◆

I went back down around 4, and stayed til 5. Normally 5 is horsie dinnertime, but they were up in the pasture. Still, I decided to leave anyway because his screaming was truly difficult to deal with. Some days I can handle it with no problem, but others... more of a problem. And I don't know why. I wasn't in a bad mood or anything. The noise just grated on my mind more than usual. To be able to leave, I went into his room to coax him in. He followed, and talked and talked in the most adorable manner. So I changed my mind and decided to stay. I left his room and allowed him to follow, thinking the screaming session was over so we could go play games now. We played for maybe 2 minutes, and then he did his dance and scream on the floor, and then was back to climbing up on top of the gate and screaming. So I lured him back to his room. He talked and talked, very expressively complete with wing motions. But I told him I loved him, closed the door and left anyway. Went upstairs and got food ready for the horses.

I went back down after feeding the horses, hoping for a better interaction since he was quiet. Instead I got one that was actually worse. I don't know why, but he would not stop screaming. Could it still be the eggs? I was down with him for maybe 10-15 minutes when I called it quits. He went into his room, I followed and checked everything to prep for bedtime. He rolled the weight to me. I rolled it back. He stopped it with his foot, then walked away from it and went under his cage instead of rolling it back to me. I told him I was going to leave him for the night. He peeked out, but didn't come out. I left him for the night. All was quiet. It must have been the eggs.

◆ ◆ ◆

When I got him down from the round pen gate and onto my shoulder, we walked over to the wood pile and I grabbed a nice-sized stick as a toy for him. We took it into the basement. Once inside he immediately took it from me when I handed it to him, and began throwing it around. Then he picked it up and took it into his room, placing it in his 'under the cage' man cave. It has been weighed, it has been measured, and its worthiness has been decided. Cool new toy.

I did some cleaning in his room, scrubbing the floor and walls, and sweeping up anything that had poo sprinkles on it. He was in there with me, rolling the weight at me, and standing in front of me talking and leaning up to me for a kiss – trying to distract me. But he did let me clean.

We played in the basement for a long time – right up to 4 actually. He was playing normally for quite awhile, and snuggling frequently. Then suddenly he got this surge of energy, and he rolled his small weight around, and around and around, and around... not even bringing it to me – just rolling it all by himself all over the basement. He brought it to me occasionally, but not til close to the end of the visit. He was terribly winded, but I couldn't get him to slow down. I got some of it on video, but of course he slowed down because he was being filmed – he'd slow down or stop and just stare at the camera.

After horse dinner I went back to Benji's room. We had a blast yet again. He was super playful and lovable. He requested so many kisses – it was crazy.

Every few minutes he would swing by and lean in for a kiss. At one point I leaned in to kiss him, and he made his little snuggly noises, and seemed to absolutely adore the affection. He danced a lot, ran around, played with his weight and metal pole mostly. He seemed so happy all the time. When it was finally time for me to leave, he looked so sad about it. But he didn't make a fuss.

Hard to believe yesterday was so screamy.

I learned something today, that I've known for quite some time and did sort of "by nature," but did not solidify until today. When I start out the visit by cleaning up and putting his food dish out etc., allowing him to go outside the room on his own, it takes longer for us to bond, or snuggle. But if I start out the time by letting him climb on my shoulder immediately, and then snuggle in the play space before playing, we have a much better time. This was brought to mind today when he waited quite awhile before snuggling with me. We had been playing and playing, and I realized, we hadn't snuggled at all. So I said something to him about it. I just said something simple, like, "We haven't snuggled yet, and I'm sad about that." Weirdly, he came over and snuggled with me.

They say that touch is bonding, and with horses, you should do a bit of grooming, or just hanging out with them before you halter, harness, or saddle them up for an activity. That bonding time is crucial to having a smooth session together to do whatever it is you're going to do. I'd say that falls into play with Benji as well. Snuggle first, and we have a better time together than if we skip the initial snuggle time.

At the end of the night, he climbed up on his cage and talked to me from the top. I talked back to him, gave him kisses etc. Then he started singing, and I sang back, trying to replicate his sounds. It seemed to astound him at first, and he quickly found it amusing. He'd sing, I'd try to sing it back while he watched me with an amused eagle eye. We did this over and over until we were done. Then he climbed on my shoulder and danced.

◆ ◆ ◆

He went into a crazy screaming wing-flapping fit on the side of his cage, but I'm not sure why. Sometimes he uses that to let me know he wants to go to bed. So I left the room and closed the door. He stopped, and said, "You come back here." (He learned that phrase from when he dances away from me as I'm trying to wipe peanut butter off of his beak.) This was followed by "Be right back!" Both were stated with some clarity, volume, and insistence. I went back, and he was fine. Climbed down the cage and we played some more. I tried to leave a bit later, and he let me know he was sad about it with U2 chatter, so I didn't go. I stayed another 10 min or so. When I finally left, he was okay with it. I think it's because I put Kenny G on, and he enjoys that for sleepytime.

◆ ◆ ◆

He screamed only once, and it was short - I played the little xylophone and he stopped. He climbed up on the gate, and I gave him the stick so he could play it too. He held it and I brought the instrument up for him to play. He tapped it once, and then dropped the stick on to it. I praised him and told him he was very musical. Yes, I lied. I'm hoping eventually I can get him to "play" it rather than just drop stuff on it.

I complained the other day about how I can generally not get anything done when I'm down there, and it is true, and it does frustrate me – but only because I really need the place to be at least somewhat clean and that takes a lot of effort. The messes this little guy can make are mind-boggling. Anyway, as we were playing yesterday and today, it really sunk in (again) that this is his time. He sits alone all day, and this is his time for company. I've been doing things, visiting with others, yadda yadda blah blah. But I'm it – all he has – so if he needs to nip at my heels to remind me of this, I should not be upset with him. I should be upset with myself for making him feel he has to do that. This is something I need to remind myself of now and again. Like now, in this journal.

◆ ◆ ◆

Vet appt day. I packed our usual travel bag of treats (walnuts and pecans), paper towels, wet wipes, and a small bag in which to put the waste. Had to leave at 930, and actually did – at 925 actually. Made a playlist of his favorite relaxing music in case he needed calming. Did not have to use it. He was grand. Had the carrier on my lap. He screamed a bit on the way there, talked a bit, did the blender sound. Inside the carrier he kept reaching for my hand, which broke my heart. But I could see he was fine. I think he also finds some comfort in seeing Howy over in the driver's seat.

Once at the vet's, he wasn't crazy about the things happening to him, but he was very good other than a couple hisses and some angry gnawing on the towel he was wrapped in. Climbed up on vet's shoulder, did his dance. Dr and assistant both thought he was playing peek a boo, so this dance must not be as common as I thought it might be. It's definitely not peek a boo. Guess it's just a Benji thing.

B's health checks out very well. His vitamin intake is stellar, his weight was a bit less than last visit due to all of the exercise he gets. When B hissed, it gave Dr H the chance to look inside his mouth. Dr H checked his beak, his ears, his cloaca, and his crop. All good. His heart rate and respiration were good, and his lungs sounded good. They then trimmed his nails, which he HATED. He gnawed very angrily on the towel, but he didn't bite anyone. They seemed to like him a lot, and they're very good with birds.

When we were paying, I looked around for something I could buy that he could play with on the way home. Couldn't find anything. Asked if I could take one of the free pens, and told them why. Wanted to ask because I felt badly taking a pen that would soon be nothing but pieces of broken plastic. I gave it to him after taking the ink cartridge out. The two assistants there looked around and thought hard about other things that B could play with on the way home. It was cute. He did chew on the pen, and had it dismantled in less than a minute.

He kept chewing on his toes... I could see that the ends of each one seemed a lighter color so I thought he was stepping in the bit of poo in there. But looked more closely and think the color may have been different from having them trimmed with the dremel tool. I put a paper towel on the bottom of the carrier to catch any more poos, and he climbed down off the perch and ripped it to shreds. I gave him another, same thing. It served as a great distraction for him, and it protected him from stepping in the poo he dropped right after we left the vet's. Must make mental note of that. He went through 3 paper towels on the drive home, and that included a stop at Starbuck's drive-thru. I asked for a stirring straw at the drive-up window, and I gave it to B. He liked it. I don't know if it's just that he knew we were going home, or if the paper towels served as a very strong happy distraction – either way, it was an awesome trip home. Not one scream. He did have some trouble staying on the perch, as he wasn't used to his new shorter claws. So he mostly stood on the floor of the carrier instead.

On the way home, we stopped for corn at a farm stand, and I took B in his carrier with me to pick out the ears. There was no one else there, so nothing to make him scream. He got to look around the countryside, and the inside of a barn shed (where the corn was on a picnic table next to a box in which you put your money). Once home, he climbed onto my shoulder, we went to his room, and he immediately climbed all the way up to his perch for a nap. The adventure fatigued him.

◆ ◆ ◆

I broke up the tall weeds I had pulled for him yesterday, so they were shorter and less intimidating in his room. I put the shorter versions in his room, tucked into his shoe rack so that they were standing upright. He went over to them to tear them up a bit. When he was done, we were back out in the play area, and I chucked the bottom of one of them like a javelin, out to the compost pile. It made it all the way there. I turned and looked at Benjamin and said, "I'm pretty good at that." He said, "Pretty good at that."

We played a lot, laughed a lot, and played different games. We were standing at the door with B on my shoulder, looking out at the relatively cold day. It was only about 60 degrees, so I figured it was too cold for him. I put him back on the gate, and sat down next to him. He sat there, looking longingly outside. I said, "Do you want to go outside?" He bobbed up and down, the way he does when he's saying yes. So I stood up, held out my hand, and he climbed on. We went outside, and stood next to the door, listening to the music playing in his room. We watched a crane fly overhead, very close to us. Benji kept his eye on it for the entire flight. I decided to go sit on the bench by the roundpen. I walked slowly to see if he was showing signs of being too cold. He did his little "bend" forward like he does when he's anxious for something. We got to the round pen gate and he climbed on.

He hunkered down and watched the world go by, and I sat on the bench and
watched him.

◆ ◆ ◆

I finally got Benji into his room and ready for bed. I put him on top of the
cage, and he did his "don't leave now" Cockatoo chatter. Then he did
something very odd. He stood tall and thin, with his crest up, and he made
this low guttural sound that I can't even find the letters to write. I'd never
heard it before. He made the sound three times. I stood watching him, and
asked him what was wrong. I moved closer, petted his head, and calmed him
down. He calmed quickly, hunkered down and did his quiet chatter for a bit
while I wrapped my arms protectively around him and hugged him.
Stretching tall like that, with feathers pulled in, is supposed to be frightened
body language, but when frightened, the umbrella is down – not up. So this
stance was a dichotomy of communication as far as I could tell. I could see
nothing anywhere that would warrant fear, or anything really. Just his room.
I glanced out the windows and didn't see anything strange out there either - at
least not by then.

When he seemed calm again, I gave him kisses and told him I'd come back to
see him in the morning, and I quietly left. He talked rapidly and loudly as I
headed upstairs. I don't know what all that was about... I felt a bit like a
mom leaving her child alone in their room when there was a monster under
the bed.

◆ ◆ ◆

I headed back down around 420ish. He was very happy to see me. No "hi
baby," but I could hear him climb down off the cage and grab his weight as
soon as he heard me close the basement door. He climbed onto my shoulder,
and I walked to the outside door. We stood and looked out for a minute. I
opened the door, and he was able to see that it was raining. He gave me a
"don't you dare" look, so I didn't... we just stood in the doorway. I told him
to look at the rain, and wasn't it beautiful. He turned his back to the outside.
He did not find rain beautiful. I laughed and closed the door. We went to the
play space and I set him down. We played for a long time. He climbed up
the ladder at one point, and screamed until I walked over to him. I gave him
a big hug and a kiss, and he climbed on my shoulder. We went to the back

part of the basement, and he let me work on dividing up the DVDs while he gnawed on a box.

When he'd had enough of that, he stood waiting for me to get him – the box was too high for him to get down. I put my hand out, and he climbed on. We went back to the ladder, and I set him on top. He left the ladder immediately, climbed back on my shoulder, and looked at the couch, so I set him on the couch. He climbed down off the pillows to the seat, and waited for me. I sat down and we snuggled for a long time – maybe half an hour. When he was done with that, he wanted to roll the weight around for awhile. He ate some sunflower seeds, played with the gate poles, snuggled on and off. I put him to bed around 640. He went to bed very easily.

◆ ◆ ◆

He must have played on the ground in the weeds for a good 20 minutes, digging up weeds and soil. I was sitting on the bench, facing him, with my bare feet on the lowest rung of the round pen gate, and my arms and head resting on the rung second from the top, sort of draped over the roundpen gate panel. I literally just sat there and watched him the entire time. Barely looked anywhere else. But at one point my mind began to drift. I was still watching him, but I was thinking about some winter prep issues for the horses that I was trying to solve.

Still looking at Benji, but mind elsewhere, I notice that he suddenly stops playing and has a weird look to him. The only way I can describe it is to say it was like an evil frown with eyebrows furrowed – and yet Cockatoos cannot create an evil frown with eyebrows furrowed. They have no eyebrows, nor will a beak frown. He drops the piece of manure he was about to throw, and makes a beeline for me... I don't think too much of it, but then I see that he's about to bite my toe! I pull my foot back away from him and he just gets a little nip on it. He angrily climbs up the rungs of the gate, gets to the top, and flaps his wings, about to scream. I stand up and ask him what the heck is going on. He leans toward me, flapping his wings again, mouth open. I take a step back, and he keeps going.

I left, and went inside the basement to get a bottle of water and give him a minute to cool down. He wanders the pen a bit more, making cute noises. I stay over by the door to the basement, leaning on the door frame, and just watch him. Maybe 2 minutes pass, and he begins to try to get back down off the pen. It's not difficult, he does it almost every day. But it seemed to flummox him this time. He wound up on the bench – taking great pains to get there. Once on the bench, he had no way down, so I figured he'd go back to the gate. He did not. He paced on the bench, back and forth and back and forth, looking at the ground, and looking at the gate. I finally went over, put my hand out, and let him climb on. I put him down on the ground, and walked back to the doors. He followed. We went inside, and he seemed fine.

No idea what that was about.

We went outside right away, but it was cloudy, and sticky, and windy. Strange weather. We walked up to the front yard and went inside so I could add water to the horses' food. I did so, and then let B drink from the faucet, as he so loves to do. He drank and drank and drank. I set up the pitcher underneath to catch all of the water that poured out of the faucet while he drank, and in between his drinks. I dumped the pitcher of water into the horse food. When B was done, I set him down on the counter and cut up half a watermelon. B stood and watched for a short while, and then wandered the counter top. I kept an eye on him. He was fine, right up to the point where he pulled a miniature Reeses peanut butter cup out of its bag and began unwrapping it. I got it away from him, put him on my shoulder, and we went back downstairs.

We played with a few toys, and I cleaned his room a bit – just the basics: water bowls, top of cage, under cage, and poos. While we were rolling weights, he wandered away, and went to the couch. I followed, sat down, and grabbed his baby blanket. He climbed onto my lap and I covered him up. We stayed like that for about half an hour. It was 515 when he got down, and I coaxed him into his room so I could go feed the horses. While feeding them, we also dumped the trailer, and I took a manure rake to pick up the horse poo pile in front of the basement doors. Two of the horses had gotten out last night, and apparently they went looking in the basement door windows. While I was picking that up, B screamed mercilessly. He saw me. I was hoping he wouldn't, because I knew it would make him scream.

Back at 615. He was over on the shelving unit, looking out the window. He climbed excitedly onto my shoulder, and we went to the play space. We played with many toys, and snuggled just a little bit. The one time we snuggled, he yawned, so I knew he was tired. When he's tired, one has to be careful with him... So I was on alert. I cleaned the gym mats with cleaner and a rag. He ran around trying to distract me. I still played with him. Scrub, scrub, roll the weight, scrub, scrub, comment on whatever he's doing, scrub, scrub, roll the weight...

My hands felt dry after being in the water, and without really thinking about it, I put some hand lotion on when I was done scrubbing. A few minutes later B came over and licked my finger. I rubbed his beak, cuz he likes that, forgetting the fact that I had just put lotion on. The lotion got onto his beak - not much as I had rubbed it into my hands well. At first he was fine with it. A couple of minutes later though he sort of zoned out – like he was trying to figure something out. Then he began screaming. I worried it was the lotion, so I grabbed a clean fluffy sock I'd brought down to use as a dusting cloth. It's super soft. I used it to rub down his beak. He immediately stopped screaming, and just sat there enjoying the soft sock being rubbed on his beak. He was fine then. We played a bit more. Around 645 he kept going for the hole he had made in the door frame, and I'd keep telling him no. Two times in a row. And each time I'd say no, he'd yell at me. He did this twice earlier in the day as well. I told him he was getting cranky now, so it was time to go to bed. I went in to make sure everything was in order, put on one of his sleepytime CDs, and closed the door. He was fine with it. No extraneous chatter, or words after I left.

◆ ◆ ◆

I went down at 10 a.m. We played with the weight, went through a box of old toys, cleaned out a closet full of Benji stuff. As long as I include him and make things fun, he's generally been okay with it these days. He had a good time looking over all of his things. At almost 11 we went back to playing with the weight, and he got all riled up again for some reason. After rolling the barbell back to me, he bit my toe again. I have no idea what this is about! I told him "no" and that he was going into a time out. I put him in his room, and closed the door.

I went back down at 2. We played just fine. A bit more work in the closet, snuggled on the couch for a long time, and then went outside. It had rained all morning, and the sun came out for the first time while we were on the couch. We went out to enjoy it – though it didn't last long. It was too windy to be out without sun, and the sun kept hiding. I'd say we were outside for no more than 10-15 minutes. Once back in, he rolled me his weight, inside his room, 3 times. Then he propped it up on its side, said something to me, and stood there. I said "Did you want to take a nap?" He said something again, and went under his cage. I left him and he took his nap.

Rainy all day, so no outside play. We reignited his interest in some old toys. I brought down the basket of toys from the kitchen play space and put it down in the middle of the room. I went through it with him, pulling each toy out and sharing it with him. There was a small plastic bag of itty bitty hard plastic pacifiers meant as decoration for a baby shower, and he spent a lot of time with that. He would rip through the bag with his beak and pull out each individual pacifier through each tiny hole, and then throw it or drop it. Once done, I put all of the pacifiers into a small red bowl. He pulled them out of the bowl individually and threw them around the room. I put some back into the torn up bag and gave it to him. He did the same – ripped and pulled and tossed. When he got to the last one, he kept wrapping it up in the bag, chewing on it, pulling it out, wrapping it up again, working it out then putting it back in.

A very nice day. We went outside for what I thought would be a brief time, as it was super windy. There was some sun, and it was very comfortable in the sun, even with the wind – though the wind blows B's feathers around a lot. I can't imagine that's comfortable. He doesn't have the top coat of feathers that sort of keeps everything nice and neat and in place, so the feathers that are there are very loose in how they move in the wind. He spent most of the time snuggled up to me. I decided to go see if it was any less windy by the pine trees. It was much better, and Benji almost jumped off my shoulder to go run around underneath the pines. We stayed there for a very long time.

Howy went out onto the front porch, and I called up and waved to him. B climbed onto my shoulder and we walked up to go spend time with Howy on the front porch. It was very nice. H brought out some watermelon, and B ate 2 pieces, then sat quietly on the back of the bench.

He spent some time facing the picture window and looking at himself, or watching tv - I don't know which.

♦ ♦ ♦

Got good footage as an example of the day. Lots of playing on his milk crates. Seemed to mostly enjoy throwing the stick, but wasn't choosy. His mood was back and forth today, but mostly good. Seemed to improve as the day went on. https://youtu.be/cCNyACDR3jI

♦ ♦ ♦

The day seems to be off for almost everyone. Our cat, Sheba, is quiet, Howy's not feeling well, and I feel mildly drained. The horses all seem good though. Anyway, I went down to see B around 11 and we had a lovely time. Played, bit of snuggles, and I got some hilarious video. But I had to go make lunch at 1210, so I left him at the height of his being adorable. Not a bad thing though, as he usually naps around noon.

When I went back to see him at 4, after we had lunch and did some major "pre-winter" chores, it kinda sucked. Benji's in a mood now. Cranky. Ate a piece of mac and cheese, played for about 2 seconds, then just roamed around

looking for something to do. Decided to just climb the gate and scream.
Then got down and screamed on the floor. Then back up on the gate. More
screams. I tried to get him interested in a few things, then finally put him in
his room, turned on the Caribbean CD he enjoys, and left him. He was quiet,
then screamed for a minute maybe 4 min after I got upstairs. Then nothing.
I'll try him again later.

I went back down after horse dinner. It was about 530. I stayed for an hour,
and we had a nice time. I took him outside right away. It was about 56
degrees, and there was wind at 8mph. I didn't want to take him out, but was
desperate to change his mood. He actually enjoyed himself out there! I think
I was colder than he was. But he was bored inside, and this seemed to help.
He climbed onto the round pen right away, roamed around for a few minutes,
and then went down to the ground to play in the wood shavings. He threw
shavings, he threw poo, he then went over to the new piles of old hay that we
added this afternoon, and started pulling pieces of hay out of the piles.

We went in and played with the weights, and some posts. He climbed the
gate a lot, complained a little, rolled the weights and poles, worked on some
pacifiers in a small bag, tried to get at the stored cars... He is determined to
get to the cars...

◆ ◆ ◆

Cranky Benji. Screaming, complaining, bored, annoyed. Second visit
slightly better than first, but only slightly. He vexes me...

◆ ◆ ◆

Was down from 11 to 12, and we were able to go outside, which was
fantastic. It was a bit chilly, and a bit windy, but we put our heads down and
powered through. He didn't want to go onto the round pen gate, which is
unusual – I think it might be the first time that's happened. We spent most of
the time sitting on the bench on the front porch. We ate some watermelon.
Then we went to the pines and he dug up dirt under the trees. He came over
to check in with me a couple of times while playing. He'd sit on my legs,
snuggle a bit, and then go back. Sat on my shoulder for the final check in,
and then let me know it was time to go. I tried to sit on the round pen bench,
and he sat with me for a brief minute, then got down and headed inside. I

took a video of him walking away because I get a kick out of his little wiggle-waddle.

After lunch, I went down again around 330 and stayed til 6. Lots of random play. Some couch snuggling, which was eventually ruined by a fly that kept dive-bombing him. Tried to go outside, but he didn't want to be out there. He went onto the dome, then climbed down and wanted to go inside. Once inside, he made it over the barrier gate, and down the other side into the car space. I wasn't looking, so I don't know how he did it – consequently I cannot fix the issue. He pulled a cap off the air nozzle on one of the tires. He was over there for all of maybe 10 seconds, and damage was done. Amazing. He dropped the cap smack dab in the middle of the space underneath the car. I had to belly crawl underneath to get it.

I'm worried about winter. He seems bored with everything except going outside, and even that isn't a happy place for him everyday (this afternoon for example). And going outside won't be an option in a couple of weeks.

◆ ◆ ◆

Had a very nice morning with him. Lots of random play. It was sunny and warm outside but I was unable to get him to go out. The clock is ticking on outside time, so it worries me when he won't go out. We played and snuggled for over an hour before I went upstairs for lunch.

I was going to head back down at 3. I thought it was strange that starting around 230 he began incessant screaming. Obnoxious screaming. Non-stop screaming. I didn't want to go down and encourage the behavior by showing up while he screamed, so I tried waiting until he stopped. At a few minutes after 3 he took a break, so I went down. He was on the shelf by the window instead of on top of his cage. He mostly uses that shelf when he looks out the window. He said "Hi Baby" when I went into his room, and he was quiet, so I thought all would be well. But as soon as I set him on the gate in the play area, he began screaming. He climbed down, and went to the door windows. I looked out and didn't see anything unusual. And then I did. A big ol' harvester came rolling on through in the pasture next door. I went into his room and put a paper towel in between his screen and window, then closed the window, so when he looked out from the shelf, he couldn't see the harvester. Figured I'd leave him alone while they did their work, and then bring him out when they were done. It didn't work. Since he couldn't watch, and yell at the harvesting from the shelf, he climbed onto the top of his cage, so he could see out the upper half of the window, which I had not covered. He outsmarted me - again...

Unfortunately the harvesting takes a lot longer than the cutting – which they did the other day. That took less than an hour. Harvesting requires baling the hay, and then bringing in more vehicles to gather up the bales, and more vehicles onto which they pile the bales. It's gonna be hell.

Been an hour now, and he's been screaming the entire time. I need to get shades of some kind for the doors to the outside. Maybe blinds – something that won't be shredded by a bird... It was nice when I could take him upstairs – he can't see the neighbor's pasture from there. But now that we've taken down the dining room barricade, it's not safe for him to be up here. Not safe for the house, that is. I can't take him outside due to the harvesting. I can't bring him upstairs due to lack of safe places for him to play. I can't take him to the back of the basement, since he knows the harvesting is happening and even if he can't see it from back there (which I think he still can), he won't stay back there. So I am left to leave him in his room for longer than I'd care to, and I am left to leave him alone since my presence does not help anything. He will still scream – constantly. Not the day I had imagined.

I went to Benji at 520. The last of the harvester people were pulling out of the field. YEA! I let Benji out, and he climbed onto the gate to suspiciously stare out the windows, looking for big scary machines. There were none. So we played! And we had fun. And we snuggled. And I got to pet him while he sat on the gate playing with his feathers. It was a relief. Then one of the machines became slightly visible over by the neighbor's house. It was so far away, just slipping into a place to park, and B had to scream about it. I distracted him, the machine stopped moving, more distraction, and in time he forgot that he could still see it.

I brought in the big box of styrofoam. I laid it on its side, and opened the end. He excitedly talked while I got it set up, and ran inside it as soon as he could. He chewed on some pieces for awhile, and then popped out with a beak covered in tiny styro balls. I love that polka-dot beak look. I then went out and got the new shelf, and set it up temporarily next to the box, and he used it as a way to chew on the box. He chewed on the box itself in several areas, on the flaps, and on the straps. I deliberately chose a box with straps because I knew he'd enjoy chewing on on those.

He went on a screaming spree. I don't know what caused it. I thought it might be a happiness screaming spree, but it had more edge than lilt, so I wasn't sure. I went to his room, with the plan to put him to bed. Instead he danced into the room, talking and sort of flapping his wings. I'm pretty sure he knew what was up so he put on his best face. We played in his room for quite awhile. After maybe 20 min he started getting super hyper, throwing things, climbing up my shoulder and dancing, which he's not supposed to do, and getting clumsy. Singing, talking, flapping, doing his exaggerated wing display, and just generally having fun – so much so that he was getting dangerous. I left the room, and he followed. He climbed onto the gate, and started to scream. I said with a somewhat forlorn tone, "Please don't." He looked at me, held the stare for a moment, and then sang instead.

He went to bed shortly thereafter, and he did so just fine.

While he was chewing on the boxes, I went into his room to move a corkboard I had gotten for him today. While in there, he said a few things while running around in the play space, and then I heard him clamor down the metal shelves. I left his room and wound up meeting him at the doorway of his playhouse. He looked me up and down, suspiciously. I'm pretty sure he would have frisked me if he had hands. He ran into his room, looked around, and then came back out. He had to make sure I didn't take or move anything important. Such a character.

By around 6 he just walked around getting into trouble, chewing on things he knew he wasn't supposed to chew on – mostly his door and the door jamb. At 615 he was screaming a lot. He ran into his room and screamed some more. I told him if he didn't quiet down I was going to have to put him to bed early. He screamed about that. So I left the room and closed the door. I turned off the lights, and turned on some piano music. He didn't make a peep.

The hardest part about spending time with Benji is finding enough to keep him interested and busy. The second hardest part is leaving him.

♦ ♦ ♦

Went down at 345 and stayed until 645. We had a very nice afternoon.
Some highlights – He's still suspiciously walking around the back basement,
and he acts as if he saw something move when I don't see anything. He
jumps, or startles, but when I look around I don't see what made him jump.

Another: While he was working diligently on the big boxes, chewing away,
he was able to get to the aluminum corner protector on the wall, and pull it
off - which was annoying. I did leave him alone there for awhile, so I could
go put the mattress protectors on. I had about 6 inches of the cover on, and
Benji came running over. He climbed up onto the gate and shuffled over to
where I was working on the mattress. As I'm pulling and tugging on the
cover, and the mattress, he started sort of doing the same on his end, with his
beak. At first I just assumed he was chewing on the mattress. So I asked him
to stop. I went back to work, and so did he. I asked him to stop again. Then
the next time, I took a moment to look at him, and saw that he wasn't
chewing, but was pulling with all of his tiny might, trying to move it, just like
I was. So I thanked him for his help, and kept working.

I moved the mattress away from the wall. It's a big fat queen size memory
foam mattress, so it's really difficult for one person to move. I had it in a sort
of bent shape, and was pulling the cover on while holding the mattress itself.
Benji came down from the gate, ran over to me and the mattress, and began
pulling on the cover with his beak – actually pulling it along so it was up
further on the mattress. Damn he's cute. It made it all even more difficult
since now I had to be sure the mattress didn't fall onto the floor, and
subsequently onto B. But the adorability of what he was doing could not be
denied.

We were laying down some soil concrete in the paddock today and had no
idea how long it was going to take. So I made sure I spent at least an hour
with B this morning. For what I believe is the first time ever, we spent the
entire hour on the couch, just snuggling. He hunkered down on my arm and
other than rearranging now and again, he didn't move. I was the one who
finally called it, got up, and put him in his room. He went in peacefully.
What an enjoyable morning, just snuggling with Mr B.

Afternoon was also enjoyable, though other than some lap snuggles on the

floor, it was almost entirely active. Lap snuggles were short and sweet. He
loves the wire clothes organizer I brought down. I pulled it from the garage,
where it held our winter coats, boots, etc, and left it outside the basement
door around 7 this morning. Dragged it in that afternoon. I think he even
tried to help, as he did with the mattress, but he may have also been simply
chewing on it. I laid it on its side so I could wipe it down. B climbed onto it
and began chewing on the plastic bits. When he got down, I started dragging
it to its place, and B ran alongside sort of grabbing it with his beak and
walking with me. Such a helpful boy.

Once it was in place against a concrete wall where nothing else could be
destroyed, he climbed on and stayed on it for easily half an hour.
https://youtu.be/Fa_y4l9_enE

He chewed and chewed and chewed on the plastic. The tiny fragments of
black plastic on the floor all over the space looked like a terrifying bug
infestation. He dangled upside down for most of the time, getting around that
way extremely well. Up until then, I've only seen him go upside down
accidentally. He did take a couple of bites out of the panel of insulation that I
thought was out of his reach but apparently was not.

◆ ◆ ◆

We tried to go outside. He really wanted to be out there. But the wind was
so strong. I sat down by the basement door, in the grass, and let him decide
what he wanted to do. He sat with me for awhile, and then climbed off my
shoulder and walked to the round pen. It was a difficult walk for him, due to
the wind. He stumbled now and again and the wind was blowing his feathers
around like crazy. He climbed up to the top, pooped, and then roamed. I
walked over and sat on the bench. He put his foot out, and I offered him my
arm. He snuggled up in my arms, and we sat there for a short while. The
wind picked up even more, so I turned to block the wind from him. We sat

there for a few minutes, but then I decided to take him in. The wind wasn't dying down, and the clouds had completely covered the sun.

During the final portion of our evening together, I asked Howy to fasten the corner protector to the wall, because once on the shelves in that space, B kept pushing it off the wall. He came down and put 2 screws into it, and it held into place beautifully. Benji kept going after it, in between chewing off small pieces of plastic on the shelves. After about the 4th try, B got angry. He stomped around on the top shelf screaming mercilessly. After 5 screams, I would do something to attract his attention, and he would stop and then go back to chewing on the plastic shelves. After awhile he would try the corner protector again, and scream when he couldn't get it to move. I'd let him scream a bit, stomp around, throw his tantrum, then I'd distract him, and he'd go back to the plastic shelving. This happened over and over. Finally I'd had it with his tantrums. I wanted to put him to bed, but couldn't get him to climb onto my arm. He was on the top shelf the whole time, and I even went and got a stepladder so I could offer him a firm perch, since I worried that it being a downward angle was why he wouldn't climb on. But no, he wasn't climbing on because he didn't want to get down.

One more tantrum and I walked over, hands on hips, and I said, "This has to stop. You are being way too loud." He struck his exuberant 'wings out and chest up' stance a few times. I laughed. He went back to chewing. Another tantrum, I walked over again and told him I'd had it. If he could have smiled, he would have. He said, "Hi baby" in his sweetest voice. I said hi baby back. He said, "Pretty bird..." I said yes, you are a beautiful boy, but you're too loud. He stepped onto my outstretched arm, and we walked over to look out the window at all of the tees bending in the intense wind. We saw a cat run by and Benji sang. Then I put him to bed. He was fine with it.

◆ ◆ ◆

When I got back from feeding the horses – he screamed the entire time I was gone - I went back down and let him out. He rode around on my shoulder for awhile, and we danced to the Zingaia "Soles on Earth" CD. I bopped up and down, and he bopped up and down on my shoulder. We looked out the window, watching the horses in the pasture while we danced. Then he suddenly screamed bloody murder while on my shoulder. I put him onto one of the shelves, and he continued to scream. And scream, and scream. He moved over to the gate, and screamed. I tried to comfort him. I gave him pets, and the screaming turned into singing. That was nice. He sang and sang and sang. At one point he developed a new dance.

Then he continued to scream again - non-stop. He kept looking outside so I finally looked out and saw that what might be the problem. There was something in the tree outside the window. It was either a nest that was hidden in leaves before (most of the leaves have blown off the tree in the intense winds), or a bunch of dead leaves that haven't yet fallen. Either way, it looks like a hawk. B screams when he sees hawks and eagles in the sky, so it made sense. I tried to tell him everything was okay, but he didn't believe me. Must easily have been 15 min of straight screaming. I got his room ready, and while I was in there, he came in screaming. He stopped in the doorway, so I gave him a little nudge in, then closed the door telling him I loved him and he should have good sleep. He went in, said pretty baby, and that was it. No more screaming.

◆ ◆ ◆

We had an electrician over at 7 a.m. He needed to do some work in the basement to hook up the heater in the garage. Consequently, Benji was awakened early by the noise, and screamed. I let him scream for awhile, hoping he'd calm down, but he kept going. When he finally took a break, I let him out. I stayed with him until around 9. He was riveted by Jeff, the electrician. He walked around behind him, watched what he was doing, showed him his toys and how he played with them, and climbed onto his shoulder. He also tried to take his screwdriver. Jeff was intrigued by him, but my honesty about whether or not B would bite was a bit too much for him. He was consequently a tad nervous. I wasn't trying to scare him and I did tell him I did not *think* B would bite him. I just can't be certain. Bottom line is that B is an animal, and animals can be unpredictable.

Benji's obsession with him made me worry about what it's going to be like when the HVAC guy comes by to put in the new system for the basement. He said it's a 3 day job... Ugh. It also made me worry that I'm not enriching his life enough if he's that interested in anyone coming down to his space (sounds like such a "relationship" thing to say). But it was a guy, and B loves guys.

I went down at 2, opened B's door and he came out right away. Didn't climb on his cage to get onto my shoulder – just walked out the door. He climbed onto the gate by the cars and pooped. I went into his room and cleaned the poo around his cage. When I came back out, he was up on the couch, pulling the blue blanket off the chair and bringing it onto the couch. I went over and sat on the couch, pulled the blanket onto my lap, and he climbed up and snuggled for a little more than half an hour. He actually pulled the blanket over and waited! How adorable!!!

I tried to get him to step up from the gate at one point, so I could take him outside. It was around 40 and the sun was shining. Cold, but in the sun it was comfortable. He wouldn't step up. I became internally upset, because I still haven't learned how to train him to step up when requested. What if there were a fire, or I needed to take him to an emergency vet appt, and I needed him to step up so I could put him in his carrier? If he didn't want to, he just wouldn't. You cannot unfurl those long toes from something they want to hang on to. On a normal day to day basis it doesn't matter, but of course I worry about the what ifs.

He seemed to sense that I was upset, and he began to act a little crazy, throwing the barbell around at a very fast pace, perhaps feeding off of my irritated energy. I sat down and talked quietly to him, gave him a kiss on his head, and he calmed down. He came over, sat on my lap and stayed there, snuggling for awhile, and then sat on my knee, his beak feathers fully fluffed, saying "hey baby" and "pretty bird" in his tiniest voice – something he does at his most mellow.

B ate two chicken bones. I thought about getting some dog bones – the rawhide ones – for him to chew on. Saw this so decided not to bother - not worth risk: Do not give your birds rawhide meant for dogs, like chews, etc. Pieces of that can be bitten off, and lodge in their crops causing infections and other problems. I use rawhide lacing, or rawhide cord, tied into knots, that my birds will chew on with no problems

I don't think I wrote about this when it happened. Benji wanted some
sunflower seeds. Usually he can open the container himself, but I had the lid
on a bit tighter than usual, so it didn't pop off when he pulled it up with his
beak. I poured some smoothie into the lid of the smoothie cup, set it down,
and told him, "Have some smoothie, and I'll open the seeds for you." He
bent over and took a sip of smoothie. Usually he drinks for a minute or two,
but this time he just took that one sip. Then, he shuffled over 2 steps to stand
beside the container of seeds. I suggested he drink just a little more. He
didn't move. I realized he had me – I didn't say how many sips he had to
have of smoothie – I only said "drink some." And indeed he had "some." He
lived up to his end of the bargain, so I conceded, and opened the seed
container for him.

◆ ◆ ◆

WORDS OF EXPERIENCE FROM OTHERS

As I was learning alongside Benji, I was also reading a lot. I found a posting on a forum called PreciselyParrots.com, where parrot owners were going over the good, the bad, and the ugly of U2 ownership. I copied many of the comments into a document so I could read them at another time. I found them so helpful I am putting them here, unedited, but sadly cannot attribute each comment to their individual posters, as I did not carry their names over into the document. These are owner comments about their birds, to help you get into the headspace of someone who has already "been there." My sincere appreciation to these folks for sharing their stories with others on a public forum. We all benefit. I strongly urge people to visit PreciselyParrots.com. It is a bounty of information supplied by a group of very helpful bird owners.

Here are some of the posts I found helpful, copied from the forum conversation:

I waited five months before I made the final choice to add him to my home and when I brought him home and heard him scream for the first time, I wanted to wilt onto the floor and cry a river, asking what I had done!

True, he loves to cuddle, he thinks I am the stars and the moon...but forget it if I leave the room...he could literally scream for hours and has in the past. He will scream until his little voice starts to give out. He came to me this way but I have yet to figure out a way to stop it and he's been with me for nearly 10 years now.

We won't even talk about all the bites that I have gotten over the years...he was much worse when he was younger and I do believe that he's growing into his hormones now at twelve...wow, he just turned 12 on March 15! I'm pretty sure he has no idea that he's a bird but thinks he's a little human who is my mate.

Around six, he started pulling, and I mean literally, pulling new pin feathers out. He's now fairly bald but I still love him. This is what happens when Cockatoos don't know they're Cockatoos. I'm lucky, he does not self mutilate, but I spent at least $3000 trying to figure out why he was plucking his beautiful feathers out and never got an answer other than the fact that he's crazy and perhaps that's all it is.

I love him with or without feathers and he will have a home with me until I am unable to care for him or someone comes along who I feel can do a better job which probably will not happen, but it might. I can assure you that you can do all the research in the world and nothing will prepare you for living with these very intelligent and very sensitive and emotional birds except living with them and so many people end up failing in that department. I think it takes a very special person to take on a Cockatoo and you need to do it knowing what you're going up against...they will push every button you have and then some.

My male is a mutilator, he chews a hole through his skin into his chest and has to wear a collar when not being watched. They really dislike certain people and don't give a lot of warning for that until it's to late. If there is someone they don't like near, at all costs they will attempt to go after that person until they are caged or the person leaves.

His bite can send you to the hospital. His devotion can bring you to your knees, humbling, truly.

Owning a cockatoo is very much a double edged sword. I don't really see things as the good, the bad (and the ugly) "anymore" as they all go together and are just part of what makes up a cockatoo. Let's face it they are truly majestic creatures that worm their way deep into our hearts. But a majesty needs a lot of space, upkeep and servitude from their slaves.

They are incredibly smart and emotional. This makes them very loving birds but also magnifies the problems they can develop when not given what they need or if something is taken away. It takes very little time or effort to create a real problem with a cockatoo. It takes a *lot* of time, effort and patience to turn that problem around and quite often it does not turn around. They are creatures of habit and "change" is often a big culprit to problems.

A new parrot owner (or even owners of smaller birds) has no idea about the *depth* of the commitment and dedication it takes to look after a cockatoo. This can't be explained or learned from a book. Those that have been there know what I'm talking about. It is truly a life altering decision no different than getting married or having a child except You are the one that is going to be doing all the learning and more importantly *adapting* yourself and your home to accommodate them. In a nutshell you basically have to revolve your life around their needs......... for the rest of your life. Not a decision to take lightly especially if you are a young person. This is an unbreakable lifetime contract with no outs.

◆ ◆ ◆

They need a lot more space than people realize and most often more than most people are willing or able to provide. Cages are the source of many/most of their problems. Providing something much larger goes a long ways to avoiding those problems. I also feel they should have others of their own kind and if all possible a large aviary environment.

◆ ◆ ◆

Cockatoos do not make good pets and even less so for the average pet owner. It takes a certain personality of person to gel with them to have a long term successful relationship. That being, a calm demeanour at all times, especially during the rough times. Stability to provide a consistent way of life. Extreme tolerance and patience because they are going to push both of them to the limit at times. Finally dedication and commitment because they are going to push those to the limit at times also. No quitters.

If this is you then you'll probably do alright with time and educating yourself. If not your in for a very rude awakening and more than likely regret. To anyone considering taking the plunge, please consider adoption. There are so many in need and so few with the right stuff to make it work.

◆ ◆ ◆

I have a U2 and while I really do love him, if I had to do it all over again, I would not have gotten him. If there was a way for people who want to get a parrot to peer into a crystal ball and see the actual future of their decision and see the reality instead of the "vision" of what the future would be like, a great many of them would come to the same conclusion. I might include myself. Thank you for understanding. I wrestle between the love and the hate I feel towards this animal, something I have never experience towards any other animal companion.

◆ ◆ ◆

I love Gizmo, he is fun, has a wicked sense of humor, is not picky about what toys he likes - destroying them all with no prejudice, says I love you unlike my other birds, all while driving me absolutely insane. He never shuts up, whether it's screaming to get his way, to get attention, to make sure you know and fully understand his opinions concerning the ongoing conversation being had by someone in person or by phone, finds my husband's annoyance with him amusing - that is when he's not trying to find a way to attack hubs. Loves to sing loudly, especially if someone is trying to listen to something important, never stays put in one place for more than two seconds, has mood swings that change so fast forget trying to keep up with his body language is impossible not to mention made my own menopausal mood swings seem like a day in the park.

I also love the way every small slight he perceives whether it is real or imagined must be paid back in blood for only blood letting can right the wrong in his mind. I'm convinced he should have been named Hannabal. There are definitely reasons they call toos psycho birds.

Don't get me wrong, I love Giz with all of my heart but caring for him on a daily basis is very emotionally draining. Partly because it's hard not to ride that emotional roller coaster ride with him through each mood change and partly because it's not just Giz I'm dealing with but a family that has no desire to have to deal with Giz's "quirks".

If I had to give one piece of advice to anyone who was thinking of getting a too it would be to not only figure out if they are a too person but to make sure their family members are as well.

◆ ◆ ◆

My Caleb hates and distrusts men. He hasn't the first flight feather, he snips them all off, but to go after my son he has LEAPED off the top of his cage and fell like a stone more than six feet! He will do anything he can to get to someone he feels is dangerous. He can leap like the best NBA star! He was on the floor and leaped straight up to get my son's finger. He had a good 2 foot ground clearance from a straight leap up! Their leg muscles are just amazing.

Now my caleb may be ... um... 'concentrated' in his neurosis. But neurosis and cockatoo seems to go hand in hand most of the time. He has nervous habits, namely snipping his feathers off and chewing a hole in his chest. He considers his feathers just another toy. He will put down a fun shreddable wicker toy to snip off part of a feather to play with. To him it's much like putting down a block to play with a ball.

A word about cages = HUGE. That's the best word I can come up with. My Caleb can't tolerate a cage. I have a 48 x36 cage. It stands at least 5 feet tall. But it's still too small for him. He now lives cage-free... well a hybrid version of cage free. He has his own bedroom. The cage is in there, but the only time the doors are closed is at nite while we all sleep. I think he takes comfort in that protection. He knows, no one can sneak up on him as he's sleeping. But he MUST have control of his life to be happy. By living cage free he has that control. He can choose to sit on the cage, play in the cage, hide under the cage, play in the corner, play in the middle of the room. He has CHOICES. If you've ever been truly helpless, with NO control of your life, it is the most *frustrating* feeling. And that's what he seems to feel when he's forced into a cage. He then turns his frustration on himself. So when shopping for a cage for a cockatoo, as soon as you find one big enough, go the next size up! And if you can manage it, a cage free option is so much better for them.

Damage? Wow! He's chewed holes in rubbermaid tubs, a drill case, numerous wall moldings, and even MY OLD TAX RETURNS! He is a one bird wood chipper. A lumber mill with feathers. He goes thru 5 times the wood that any of my other birds do, including a scarlet macaw.

They are truly amazing creatures, but not for the faint of heart. you must have patience, easy going nature, and above all a sense of humor.

◆ ◆ ◆

I took zookeeping classes, and learned something all keepers have to expect: there is a good chance the animals you care for will kill you some day. If You are a keeper, you have to accept that. With cockatoos, you have to accept you will definitely get bit, hard. You might need stitches. If you aren't okay with that, maybe don't get a big cockatoo. I'm fine if I get a bad bite, I love dexter more than I am afraid of pain. It'll be difficult the first time I get a bad bite, but I won't stop loving him because of it.

◆ ◆ ◆

And finally, one of my personal favorites:

You have to possess a certain amount of crazy to be owned by a cockatoo.